KU-444-386

FIRST
FOODS

Dr. Miriam Stoppard

FIRST
FOODS

DORLING KINDERSLEY

London • New York • Sydney • Moscow

A DORLING KINDERSLEY BOOK

DESIGN & EDITORIAL Mason Linklater

SENIOR MANAGING ART EDITOR Lynne Brown
MANAGING EDITOR Jemima Dunne

SENIOR ART EDITOR Karen Ward
SENIOR EDITOR Penny Warren

PRODUCTION Antony Heller

First published in Great Britain in 1998 by
Dorling Kindersley Limited, 9 Henrietta Street,
Covent Garden, London WC2E 8PS

Visit us on the World Wide Web at http://www.dk.com

Copyright © 1998
Dorling Kindersley Limited, London
Text copyright © 1998 Miriam Stoppard

All rights reserved. No part of this publication may be reproduced,
stored in a retrieval system, or transmitted in any form or by any
means, electronic, mechanical, photocopying, recording or otherwise,
without the prior written permission of the copyright owners.

A CIP catalogue record for this book is available
from the British Library

ISBN 0-7513-0554-5

Reproduced by Colourscan, Singapore
and IGS, Radstock, Avon
Printed in Hong Kong by Wing King Tong

CONTENTS

INTRODUCTION 6

C H A P T E R

FEEDING AND NUTRITION 9

EQUIPMENT FOR WEANING YOUR BABY 10
WEANING YOUR BABY 12 • FIRST TASTES 14
FEEDING AN OLDER BABY 16 • GOOD FOODS 18
FEEDING YOUR TODDLER 20 • FAMILY AND SOCIAL EATING 22
FEEDING PROBLEMS 24 • NUTRITION 26
A BALANCED DIET 28 • FOOD PREPARATION 30
FRUITS AND VEGETABLES 32

C H A P T E R

EVERYDAY MEALS 35

RECIPE HINTS AND TIPS 36
BREAKFAST 37 • EGG AND CHEESE MEALS 42
MEALS WITH FISH 49 • MEALS WITH MEAT 54
VEGETABLE MEALS 64 • NUTRITIOUS SOUPS 74
SNACKS AND PICNICS 77

C H A P T E R

SPECIAL OCCASIONS 85

EASTER FEAST AND TREATS 86
CHRISTMAS DINNER AND TREATS 88
BIRTHDAY PARTY 90

INDEX 94 • ACKNOWLEDGMENTS 96

INTRODUCTION

There's no question that a child's diet is important because first foods and tastes form the building blocks for a lifetime of good diet and health. What your child eats shouldn't get to be an obsession with you, however. If you're anxious about it, mealtimes will become battlegrounds. Remember that babies, like animals, are self-regulating, so try to be flexible and let your child take the lead – up to a point.

EATING PATTERNS

One of the mistakes parents often make is to impose adult appetites and eating habits on children. Children's appetites are notoriously fickle; they're easily distracted from their food and they may have a fad for certain foods for days or even weeks on end. However, your child will get all the nutrients she needs if you try to think in terms of providing her with a wide variety of foods over a weekly rather than a 24-hour period. Don't get upset when she rejects a meal; she'll probably eat heartily at the next one.

From the time they can feed themselves, most children will want fairly frequent meals or snacks consisting of small amounts of food with different textures and colours. *First Foods* shows you how to arrange meals in cheerful picture-book shapes and patterns; it doesn't take a lot of time and effort but does make foods look appealing. Treat the shapes as a catalogue of ideas to encourage your child to enjoy eating, to try new foods and to have fun at mealtimes.

GUIDELINES TO HELP YOUNG EATERS

It's worth following a few guidelines when trying to tempt young eaters. Pay attention to texture. When children are teething, their gums are very sensitive and they're still learning to use their mouths, teeth and tongues. Crunchy foods served with soft puréed ones will provide good variety at this stage. Use fruits and vegetables for colour as well as for all the different nutrients they supply. With vegetables, choose a cooking method such as steaming or stir-frying as often as you can so they keep their colour and flavour, and serve some of them raw as chewy instant snacks. Remember to keep portions small so your child doesn't feel put off by the quantity. Better to give seconds than have a pile of rejected food. Always let foods cool right down before serving, since young children's mouths are particularly sensitive to temperature and can be easily burned.

SOCIABLE FAMILY EATING

Mealtimes should be relaxed, sociable and enjoyable occasions. It's important to bring an open mind to feeding children so that you don't put undue pressure on them and make mealtimes unhappy. After the initial weaning process, your child should join with family meals whenever possible to establish a pleasant routine and to learn acceptable table behaviour by following your good example. But do keep rules and restrictions at mealtimes to a minimum.

Make your life easier by using a plastic bib and putting newspaper or a plastic sheet on the floor and underneath the high chair, so you can quickly clean up jettisoned food after the meal. The sooner you let children feed themselves with fingers or a spoon, the sooner they become adept at getting the food into their mouths without too much mess. This is part of the attraction of finger foods; not only do they encourage independence and learning, they also give you and the rest of the family time to enjoy the meal.

At first, don't expect your child to be able to feed herself an entire meal. Some food is bound to end up on the floor and in the bib and you'll have to help some of the time. Mealtimes will be more fun for you too, however, if you try to allow your child some independence. But never be tempted to leave your child alone when she's eating. It's too quick and easy for a young child to choke, so always be on hand in case something goes down the wrong way.

HEALTHIER EATING HABITS

Preparing food for a young child may mean making some changes in your cooking habits. For example, don't add salt during or after cooking. Adding salt puts a strain on young kidneys and encourages a taste for salt instead of the food's natural flavour. Whenever you serve anything but fresh, raw foods, try to be aware of exactly what you're feeding your child. All the foods in *First Foods* are wholesome and free from artificial additives. Read labels on processed foods carefully. Not all "E" numbers identify chemicals, so do try to find out exactly what they stand for. Note the order of the ingredients. They're listed by quantity, with the greatest amount first. If water is top of the list, water is the main ingredient and the product won't be very nutritious. Also note the salt, sugar and gluten content of processed foods.

Cutting down on salt, sugar and saturated fats is a good idea for everyone, so perhaps this is a time in your life when you too can try to eat a more healthy, wholefood-based diet, if you don't already do so. You may be unfamiliar with some of the foods mentioned in this book. Tofu (beancurd) is one example. It can be an ideal food for babies and young children because it supplies a wide range of nutrients quickly and easily. It's tasteless and smooth in texture but when cooked it absorbs other flavours well. Experiment with tofu; you might be pleasantly surprised.

HOW THIS BOOK IS PLANNED

The first part of this book tells you all about weaning your baby and feeding an older baby and toddler, with helpful food preparation dos and don'ts. You'll find information on family and social eating, practical guidelines to nutrition and help with feeding problems, including food intolerance and allergies. Separate charts suggest when to introduce different foods to your child and give advice on preparing and serving fresh fruits and vegetables.

The second part of the book is full of wonderful ideas for feeding children from nine months old. All the meals are based on finger foods. They're nutritionally balanced and generally made with foods that you'd use and prepare for the rest of the family. Everyday Meals has ideas for breakfast, meals with eggs and cheese, fish, meat or vegetables, soups, and snacks and picnics, while Special Occasions shows you how to make healthy treats for festivals such as Easter and Christmas, and birthdays. I hope that the combination of fun shapes, nutritious ingredients and different flavours will make each one of these meals a winner every time, with you, your child and your whole family.

FEEDING AND NUTRITION

Somewhere towards the end of six months is a good time to start to wean your baby onto solid foods. Then, during the next six months, he'll move on from mere "tastes" of solids with his milk feeds to three solid meals a day.

An understanding of basic nutrition will help you to give him the food he needs for healthy growth. Learning to feed himself is an enormous step in your baby's physical and intellectual development and you should encourage all his attempts to do so. Always be flexible and introduce new foods slowly, one at a time, so that you can identify food that doesn't suit your child.

EQUIPMENT FOR WEANING YOUR BABY

For the first few months of life, breast or bottle milk will be your baby's only food, and it will provide him with all the nutrients he needs. You won't be thinking about giving your baby solid food until he is at least four months of age (see p. 12), and even then you'll need very little equipment: a bib and some spoons will do. At first you can feed him on your lap or in an infant chair. Later, when he can sit up by himself, you'll need a high chair to feed him in.

PORTABLE BOOSTER SEATS AND HIGH CHAIRS

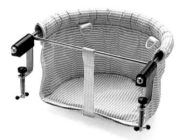

Clip-on chair
This kind of chair is suitable for babies over six months of age. Some models grip the table when the child sits in the chair; others use clamps.

High chair
Many high chairs adapt to other uses, like swings or tables. Make sure that the model you choose is stable and has washable surfaces.

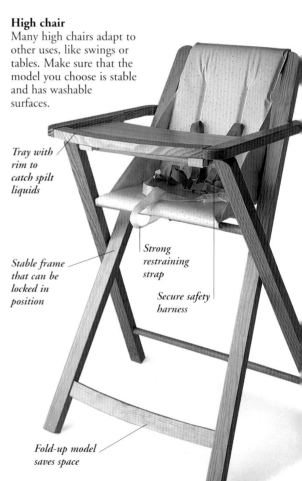

Tray with rim to catch spilt liquids

Stable frame that can be locked in position

Strong restraining strap

Secure safety harness

Fold-up model saves space

Booster seat
A child of over 18 months can reach table height with a purpose-made seat. It is more stable than a cushion and can be firmly strapped to a chair.

WHAT YOU WILL NEED TO BUY

To begin with, you'll probably feed your baby on your lap or in an infant seat, but once his neck and back muscles are strong enough to support him (at about six months), a high chair will make life easier. There is a wide variety to choose from and many convert to other uses, like an all-in-one chair and table for a toddler. Make sure the chair is stable and has washable surfaces, a tray with a rim and hooks for a safety harness. If you're buying secondhand, check the chair for general wear and tear and see that the surfaces are smooth.

You will also need equipment to mash food into a purée and an unbreakable bowl to serve it in (some come with a suction pad to secure the bowl). Special dishes that keep food hot are handy but not essential. Bibs are essential, however, as well as plastic spoons, forks and beakers.

BIBS AND FEEDING UTENSILS

Making the best choice

Choose unbreakable utensils in easy-to-wash plastic. A moulded plastic bib with a trough to catch spills is probably most efficient.

OTHER KITCHEN ITEMS

Your kitchen equipment will probably already include the other items you need.

- *A stainless-steel grater with coarse and fine perforations for preparing hard vegetables like carrots before cooking.*

- *A steamer for fast cooking to preserve nutrients. A collapsible model will fit any saucepan.*

- *Nylon chopping boards (not wooden ones, which harbour germs). Prepare vegetables and fruits, raw meats and cooked meats on separate boards.*

- *A nylon sieve and large plastic, nylon or stainless-steel spoon, or a small hand-held electric blender.*

- *Plastic containers with airtight covers for storing food in the refrigerator.*

Hand-turned food mill
When your baby starts on solids, a hand-turned food mill is a perfectly adequate alternative to a blender for mashing food into a purée.

Fine and coarse cutting discs

FABRIC BIB WITH
PLASTIC BACKING

PLASTIC BIB WITH
MOULDED TROUGH

PLASTIC BOWL

PLASTIC BEAKER

SPOON AND FORK

Your baby may be reluctant to try new foods, so give him time to get used to each food and don't persist if he seems to dislike something.

- *If your baby doesn't like taking food from a spoon, dip a clean fingertip into the food and let him suck the food off it.*

- *Use unprocessed infant cereals rather than ones that are ready mixed, and make them up in small quantities.*

- *Don't give foods containing nuts, gluten, whole cow's milk or egg until at least six months, to minimize the risk of your child developing later allergies.*

- *Give one new food at a time. Try it once and wait for several days before giving it again to see if there's a reaction.*

WEANING YOUR BABY

Somewhere towards the end of six months is a good tim to start to wean your baby onto solid foods. Four mont is a little too early, and you could leave it quite a bit lat than that. Your baby's young digestive system is incapab of processing, digesting and absorbing complex foods. solids are introduced too early, they'll pass through large undigested, and this will put an increased strain on yo baby's immature kidneys.

Milk – either breast milk or its formula equivalent – is t only food your baby needs in the early months. If a baby introduced to solids too young, it can lessen his desire suck (breastfed babies will take less milk from your breas and you'll respond by producing less milk). Either way, yo baby could end up with a diet that doesn't meet his need

WHEN TO WEAN

As your baby grows, he'll need to take in more and mo milk to maintain this growth. But your baby's stomach ca hold only a certain amount of milk at each feed; eventuall he will reach a point when he's drinking to full capacity each feed but still doesn't have enough calories for his need Your baby will let you know that he needs more to eat by change in his feeding habits. He may start to demand mo milk and appear very unsatisfied after each feed, or he m start demanding a sixth feed when he has previously bee quite content on five. A classic instance is a baby who h been sleeping through the night starting to wake for night-time feed. This is the time to introduce solids. Mar babies do this at around four months, when their inten

SPOONFEEDING
Introducing solid food
Sit your baby in an upright position halfway through his feed. Scoop up some food on a small spoon and gently insert it between his lips. Don't push the spoon in too far or your baby may gag (he may take a month or two to get used to the spoon). Once your baby has had enough, he will turn his head away.

Messy baby
If your baby pushes out more food than h takes in, gently scrape the excess onto his lip

esire to suck lessens, although it can be later. You should e aware of the signs that your baby gives you and follow is lead for the introduction of solids. The first tooth, if it ppears at or after six months, definitely indicates the need o introduce solid foods.

GIVING THE FIRST SOLIDS

Have a small amount of prepared food to hand and then ettle in your normal position to feed your baby. Although e is ready for the calories that solid foods provide, your aby will still prefer what he knows to be satisfying – milk. tart by feeding him from one breast or by giving half the sual bottle. Then give him one or two teaspoons of food. egin with the midday meal because your baby will not be avenous but will be wide awake and more co-operative. Never force him to take more food than he wants. When he's aken the solid food, give him the rest of the milk. Once he ecomes used to solids, he may prefer to take them first.

As soon as your baby is having solid food in any quantity, e will get thirsty and need water. Start with 15 millilitres ½ fluid ounce) of water or very dilute fruit juice between nd after feeds and whenever he's thirsty. Avoid sweetened rinks, since these will damage his teeth. Start with about 20 millilitres (4½ fluid ounces) of water and juice a day.

VEGETARIAN WEANING

A growing baby can get all the nutrients necessary for health and vitality from a diet that excludes meat, fish and poultry provided a proper balance of the different food groups is maintained.

- *Your baby's main source of calories will still be milk, so give this at each feed.*

- *Cereals and grains provide both carbohydrates and protein for energy and growth, while vegetables and fruits supply essential vitamins and minerals.*

- *A vegetarian diet is bulkier and lower in calories than one with meat, so your baby may get full before he's taken all he needs. To avoid this, make sure to offer a wide variety of low-fibre foods such as cheese.*

EXAMPLES OF WEANING STAGES

FEEDS	WEEKS 1 AND 2	WEEKS 3 AND 4	WEEKS 5 AND 6
1ST FEED	Breast or bottle feed.	Breast or bottle feed.	No early morning feed.
2ND FEED	Half breast or bottle feed. Try one or two teaspoons of purée or cereal and then give rest of feed.	Half breast or bottle feed. Two teaspoons of cereal or baby rice. Rest of feed.	Half breast or bottle feed. Two teaspoons of cereal or baby rice. Rest of feed.
3RD FEED	Breast or bottle feed.	Half breast or bottle feed. Two teaspoons of vegetable or fruit purée. Rest of feed.	Half feed. Two teaspoons of vegetable purée. Two teaspoons of fruit purée. Rest of feed.
4TH FEED	Breast or bottle feed.	Breast or bottle feed.	Half feed. Two teaspoons of purée. Rest of feed.
5TH FEED	Breast or bottle feed.	Breast or bottle feed.	Breast or bottle feed.

FIRST TASTES

The chart below is designed to give you an idea of when t
introduce different foods to your child. The age timings a
approximate, since children develop at such different rate
and have individual tastes. Always be flexible and use th
chart as a guide only. Introduce new foods slowly, one at
time, so that you can identify food that doesn't suit you

APPROXIMATE AGES FOR INTRODUCING DIFFERENT FOODS TO YOUR CH

FOOD	3–6 MONTHS	4–6 MONTHS	6–7 MONTHS
CEREALS	Fortified baby cereal	Non-wheat cereals; rice, oats, millets, barley, rye, soya. Cook in twice the volume of liquid	Wheat cereals, muesli, wheat products Bread, crispbreads, rusks
DRINKS	Water, apple juice	Fruit and vegetable juices, well diluted	Full-fat cows' milk
VEGETABLES	Not yet	Cooked carrots, peas, beans, marrow, swede, squash, celery, cauliflower, spinach, parsnip	Tomatoes (peeled or sieved a pulp at first) Potatoes (in addition to, no place of, other vegetables)
FRUITS	Not yet	Cooked fruits, e.g. apples, pears Ripe banana	Soaked dried apricots and o dried fruits (but avoid raisir sultanas)
DAIRY PRODUCTS	Not yet	Not yet	Full-fat cows' milk Cottage, soft and hard chee Yoghurt, plain or with puré
MEAT	Not yet	Not yet	White meat: chicken, turke Liver: chicken, calf's or lam
PULSES	Not yet	Not yet	Tofu, lentils, peas
FISH	Not yet	Not yet	White fish, skinned and bo
EGGS	Not yet	Not yet	Egg yolk only
SEEDS, NUTS	Not yet	Not yet	Not yet
LIMIT THESE FOODS		All sweetened drinks including blackcurrant syrup drinks	All sweetened drinks includ blackcurrant syrup drinks

aby. If your child rejects any new food, go back to serving
s old favourites and try offering him the new food again
ter a few days; there's no need to insist that your child
nishes the new food if he doesn't like it.

As long as you serve a variety of foods from the categories
sted below, you will be providing a good range of essential
utrients. Just try to ensure that your child eats foods from
ach of the food groups (see p. 26) over weekly periods.

KEY TO CHART

Blend or purée
Mash or mince
Soft pieces; finger foods
Larger chopped pieces;
finger foods

MONTHS	9–12 MONTHS	OVER 12 MONTHS
e grains (from 8 months)	Grissini (hard breadsticks) Wheatgerm	Once child can chew well, bread containing whole grains, e.g. granary bread
shakes	No new foods	No new foods
vegetable pieces. in large chunks at first id bits breaking off and swallowed whole	More strongly flavoured vegetables, e.g. broccoli, cabbage, leeks, onions, peppers	Salad leaves Sweet corn
ripe fruits, peeled and	Sultanas, soaked until soft (from 10 months)	Once child can chew well, leave skin on Berries, small seed fruits
shakes n yoghurt	No new foods	No new foods
red meat: lamb or beef	Meat balls, meat loaf, beefburger	Well-cooked pork without fat Processed meats, e.g. sausages
eans (from 8 months)	No new foods	No new foods
w foods	Tinned fish, well drained Oily fish, e.g. mackerel, tuna	Shellfish Smoked fish
w foods	Whole egg, whole egg products, e.g. custard (from 10 months)	No new foods
nsaturated oils	No new foods	Whole nuts only after 3 years
biscuits, fried foods eetened drinks	Butter, cream, ice cream All sweetened drinks	Processed meats, honey, sweets All sweetened drinks

INTRODUCING CUPS

You can introduce your baby to drinking from a cup when he is about four months old.

- *Beakers with spouts are best because your baby will have to half suck and half drink to get anything. Soft spouts are the easiest for a baby to use.*

- *As your baby progresses, you may find that he prefers to move on to a two-handled cup that he can grasp easily. Cups with specially slanted lips are excellent because the contents come out with little tipping.*

Two handles allow easy grip

Using a trainer cup
Lunchtime and late afternoon feeds are probably the best times to use a trainer cup, since these are the times when your baby will be more likely to eat solid foods.

FEEDING AN OLDER BABY

During his first year, your baby will move on from mere "tastes" of solids with his milk feeds to three solid meals day, plus drinks of water, diluted fruit juice or plain milk

Once he is happy with two or three different solids, it important to introduce a variety of tastes and textures. A well as being able to deal with puréed, mashed or choppe foods, he'll also learn to enjoy chewing and sucking on larg chunks of food (see p. 18), but it is important to rememb that every baby has different requirements and appetites. you are in any doubt, just feed him as much as he will tak happily. The amount of milk he requires will lessen as th number of solid meals he takes increases. Since he'll b getting most of his calories from solids rather than fron milk, your baby will become thirsty. When he does, giv him plain water or diluted fruit juice to drink rather tha milk. Nonetheless, most babies like to have a milk drin last thing at night until into their second year.

FEEDING YOUR CHILD

Until your baby is six months old, you will probably fee him on your lap or in an infant chair, but once his nec and back muscles are strong enough for him to sit up, yo may consider using a high chair or feeding table. With feeding table, you will have to bend down to feed you baby until he can feed himself, and at first you may hav to prop him up with cushions, so a high chair is probabl the better option; for his safety, make sure your baby properly strapped in at all times. Your child should alway be supervised by an adult while he's eating. Almost a children gag on some food at some stage and it is essenti that you react quickly in such a situation. A new textur taken for the first time, may make him gag simply out surprise. If he does gag or appear to choke, pat him firml on the back and encourage him to cough until the food dislodged. Talk soothingly and gently rub his back, an he'll be more able to swallow the new food.

Your baby will soon look forward to mealtimes as a opportunity to play as well as to eat, so feeding will becom messier. Place his high chair away from the walls and p newspapers on the floor in case he starts throwing foo Within a month or so of starting solids, your baby will b able to take food from the spoon.

Encourage self-feeding
Allow your child to spoonfeed himself
if he can. Choose non-runny foods,
such as porridge or thick purées.

*Moulded
plastic bib to
catch spills*

SELF-FEEDING

Learning to feed himself is an enormous step in your baby's
physical and intellectual development, and so you should
encourage all his attempts to do so. His manual dexterity
and hand–eye co-ordination will greatly improve with self-
feeding, so let him experiment if he shows an interest and
be prepared to cope with the mess.

It may be several months before your baby can really feed
himself. Help him by giving him foods that will stick to the
spoon, such as porridge, or foods he can hold (see below) if
he finds using a spoon frustrating. Food will be a plaything
and most will land on the floor rather than in his stomach.
The best way to ensure that he gets at least some food is for
both of you to have a spoon. Use two spoons of the same
colour and type so that you can swap your full spoon for
his empty one when he has difficulty scooping up the food.

FOODS FOR SELF-FEEDING

FRUIT AND VEGETABLES	CEREALS AND GRAINS	PROTEIN
• Any fresh fruit that is easy to hold, such as bananas, cut into chunks or slices with the skin or pips removed • Vegetables, particularly carrots, cut into sticks or shapes that are easy to grasp (don't cut pieces too small: your baby might choke) • Thick mashed potato	• Small pieces of dried, sugar-free cereal • Little balls of cooked (preferably brown) rice • Fingers of wholemeal bread or wholemeal rusks (not bread that incorporates complete whole grains) • Pasta shapes • Hard breadsticks	• Pieces of soft cheese, such as Gouda • Toast fingers with cheese • Small pieces of hamburger • Low-fat soft cheese spread on wholemeal bread • Any meat in small pieces • Filleted fish, such as cod, in firm chunks • Sliced hard-boiled eggs

FINGER FOODS

If your baby has difficulty using a spoon, he will find finger foods easier to handle.

Make sure wholewheat bread has no tough grains in it —

— *Pretty shapes will make food look appealing*

Cut or slice vegetables into easy-to-grasp shapes —

GOOD FOODS

Children's appetites are notoriously fickle. They are easily distracted from their food and may have a fad for certain foods for days or even weeks on end. When planning meals for your baby, try not to think in terms of a 24-hour cycle; it's more like a weekly cycle. Don't get upset when he rejects a meal – he will probably eat heartily at the next. Even if he rejects certain foods for weeks at a time, your baby is likely to get the essential nutrients from elsewhere as long as you make sure to serve a wide variety of foods (see p. 26).

Remember, a baby's stomach can't hold very much and he will need to eat more often than you do; so don't insist he finishes his meals, and be prepared to give snacks in between times. Of course, you should encourage your baby to have regular feeding times, but if you try to make him eat at meal times only, they will become battlegrounds, and he may end up by not getting the food he needs. The suggested menus below are intended as a guide to your baby's main meals.

SUGGESTED MENUS FOR AN OLDER BABY

MEAL	WITH MEAT	WITHOUT MEAT
BREAKFAST	• Rice cakes • Hard-boiled egg • Breast milk/formula	• Mashed banana • Wholemeal toast fingers • Breast milk/formula
LUNCH	• Strained vegetables and chicken • Stewed apples (skin and pips removed) • Diluted fruit juice	• Mashed potato and grated cheese • Pear slices (skin and pips removed) • Diluted fruit juice
AFTER-NOON	• Wholemeal toast fingers • Orange segments • Breast milk/formula	• Rice cakes • Apple pieces (skin and pips removed) • Breast milk/formula
SUPPER	• Cauliflower cheese • Semolina with soaked puréed dried fruit such as apricots • Diluted fruit juice	• Pasta shapes with tomato sauce • Yoghurt with fruit purée such as mango • Diluted fruit juice

FOODS FOR TEETHERS

When your baby is teething, he will like to chew and suck to soothe his gums. Any piece of raw vegetable or fruit that is large enough to hold easily and can be sucked or chewed makes a good teething food, particularly if it is chilled but not frozen really solid. Wholemeal bread crusts give your baby something hard to bite on at first and then become soft so they can be swallowed easily. If you have time, try to make your own teething biscuits and rusks; they're quick to do, inexpensive and free from unwanted additives and sugar. Most commercial varieties contain almost as much sugar as ordinary biscuits and those advertised as "low-sugar" simply disguise their sugar content in the form of glucose: not a good start for first teeth. Older children may like to gnaw on a bone, for instance a spare-rib, lamb chop or chicken drumstick, but take care not to offer anything with sharp edges, which can catch on inflamed gums. Teething can be a wearing time for everyone, but try not to resort straight away to using patent medicines and teething gels; nearly all contain a local anaesthetic that provides only a moment's relief, and they can also cause allergies.

Relieving the pain
Chewing and sucking on firm-textured foods, like the ones shown here, helps to soothe your baby's sore gums and ease the pain of teething.

TEETHING BISCUIT

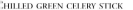

CHILLED GREEN CELERY STICK

ITALIAN BREADSTICK

PEELED CUCUMBER

OVEN-BAKED RUSKS

PLAIN OAT BISCUIT

PEELED RAW APPLE

FEEDING YOUR TODDLEF

By the age of 18 months, your baby should already be eatin more or less the same foods as you, and will probably tak about one-third to half an adult portion at meals. Mak sure he has at least one protein food at each meal and fo servings of fruit and vegetables a day. Aim to give a goo mixture of foods from the different food groups (see p. 28

Don't give your child highly seasoned or sugary food offer nutritious fresh fruit or yoghurt rather than pudding Also avoid any small, hard pieces of food that your chil could choke on, such as whole nuts or popcorn, fruit wit stones or pips or very small pieces of raw fruit or vegetable

FAMILY EATING

Now that your toddler is feeding himself, he'll enjoy sittin at the table during family mealtimes. Although he's eatin the same food as everyone else, you may need to mash c chop it so that he can eat without too much help. A ver messy eater can be fed before the rest of the family, the allowed to sit at the table with some finger foods. Difficu eaters feel encouraged to eat more at family meals.

It will be some time, however, before your child is read to sit still during mealtimes. If he wants to get down fror the table, let him go, and don't try to make him come bac to finish his food if he has obviously lost interest in it. H will make up for it by eating more at the next meal.

MESSY EATERS

Your child may regard mealtimes as just another game an why not? He'll see nothing wrong in throwing food aroun getting it everywhere. Although it may see that he is doing it on purpose, it's just phase and his co-ordination wi eventually improve (food provid the perfect motivation for speedir up your child's balance and musc co-ordination). Make mealtim easier on yourself and less stres ful by surrounding the high cha with newspaper, which ca be gathered up at the end each meal. Being tidy ca be turned into a game of i

Keeping clean
Bibs and plastic equipment that is easy to wash help to keep messy mealtimes more manageable.

wn: you could draw a circle on the tray of the high chair
show your toddler where his mug or bowl should go. If
keeps it there, give him a treat or reward (see p. 22).

MENU PLANNING

The menus below assume that your toddler will eat three
meals a day and several snacks in between times. If you find
in practice that he eats fewer meals and more snacks, just
make sure you choose snack foods that you would have
served at mealtimes, for instance Stickman Feast (see p. 77)
or Dips (see p. 79) with vegetables, fruit or rusks.

SUGGESTED MENUS FOR A TODDLER

DAY 1	DAY 2	DAY 3
Breakfast	**Breakfast**	**Breakfast**
½ slice wholemeal toast	25g (¾oz) cereal plus ½ cup milk	1 tablespoon baby muesli with 50ml (1½fl oz) milk
1 chopped hard-boiled egg	1 sliced pear, no skin	½ mashed banana
1 cup diluted fresh fruit juice	½ slice wholemeal toast	small tub of fruit yoghurt
	1 cup diluted fresh fruit juice	1 cup diluted fresh fruit juice
Lunch	**Lunch**	**Lunch**
50g (1½oz) white fish	1 beefburger in a wholemeal bread roll	1 cheese sandwich made with wholemeal bread
50g (1½oz) brown rice (dry weight)	30g (1oz) steamed broccoli	pieces of raw carrot
1 tablespoon sweetcorn	1 medium tomato	1 sliced apple, no skin
1 cup diluted fresh fruit juice	1 cup diluted fresh fruit juice	1 cup milk
Dinner	**Dinner**	**Dinner**
50–75g (1½–2½oz) cauliflower with 50g (1½oz) grated cheese	½ wholemeal bread roll	2 sardines (packed in brine or tomato sauce, not in oil)
50g (1½oz) broad beans	50g (1½oz) broad beans	50g (1½oz) baked beans
50g (1½oz) chicken, no skin	50g (1½oz) chopped liver	1 medium tomato
1 small wholemeal bread roll	50g (1½oz) wholemeal pasta (dry weight)	1 cup milk
½ banana blended with 1 cup milk	1 cup water	
Snacks	**Snacks**	**Snacks**
1 small yoghurt	1 unsweetened wholemeal biscuit	1 orange in segments
1 banana	1 rice cake	1 fromage frais
1 wholemeal bread roll	1 cup water	1 packet unsalted crisps
1 cup water	1 cup milk	1 cup diluted fresh fruit juice

TREATS AND REWARDS

Every parent knows that there are times when it is important either to reward a child's good behaviour or to offer a bribe in return for some form of co-operation.

Sweets might seem like the most suitable reward, since children always appreciate them. However, you may feel that to give sweets routinely as a reward undermines the consistency of your approach to sweet-eating in general. There is no hard and fast rule on this, and there is no reason why you shouldn't occasionally reward your child with sweets as long as you make it clear that it is a one-off gift.

It's worth making an effort, however, to devise other forms of treat or reward: a favourite flavour of yoghurt, a small toy or a new box of crayons, or an especially extended bath-time or bed-time story.

I don't believe in placing a total ban on sweets, because this can encourage children to become secretive and dishonest.

I do believe in rationing sweets, however, and this always worked with my own children. If you let your child have one sweet after lunch and one after supper, and encourage him to brush his teeth afterwards, you will be encouraging self control, good eating habits and good oral hygiene for his lifetime.

FAMILY AND SOCIAL EATING

For many families, mealtimes are about much more than making sure everyone is fed: they are social occasions when all the members of the family sit down together, exchang news and enjoy each other's company. For a small child these times form an important part of his learning process He can appreciate this social aspect of mealtimes and will learn most of his behaviour at table from his experience of family eating, rather than from any number of lectures at later age, so that the family will be able to enjoy mealtime without repeated disruptions caused by bad manners and arguments about behaviour.

As soon as your child first sat in his high chair at the family dining table, he will have been watching and learning He will want at least to try the foods that you are eating and will often join in the conversation. Try to include your child in family meals as often as possible. Give praise when he tries to follow your good example, for instance, asking for something to be passed to him instead of attempting to grab it from the other side of the table. Children learn most naturally and easily by example and will rapidly pick up the behaviour that the rest of the family observe. If everyone in your family leaves the table when it suits them, for example rather than waiting for the others to finish eating, it will be hard to persuade your child to sit still and wait.

There will be times when you want your child to behave especially well at mealtimes, usually because you are having visitors. Allow him to join in the excitement of a special meal by letting him help lay the table, perhaps. If he knows that some occasions demand an extra effort, he will find it easier to understand why you want him to be particularly well behaved and will therefore react better to your wishes

KEEPING MEALTIMES RELAXED

It is important that meals don't become a battleground for more generalized family conflict. The association between food and love can be very close, and arguments about food and eating can be associated with tensions over other issues In such cases, eating behaviour, such as a refusal to eat, can become a weapon that the child uses to manipulate you, to gain attention or to express anger, distress and many othe motions. It is best, therefore, to be fairly easy-going about table etiquette with your child, to keep mealtimes as relaxed as possible and not to be drawn into arguments. Insist only on those aspects of table manners that you consider to be essential; refinements can come later.

EATING AWAY FROM HOME

An older child will have definite preferences about what he wants to eat and indulge himself. There are likely to be occasions when your child is eating away from home and, while you obviously can't account for every mouthful he eats, it's worth trying to ensure that the good habits he learned at home are not lost once he starts to eat meals elsewhere.

If your child goes to a playgroup, nursery school or "proper" school, try to make sure he has a good breakfast beforehand. If he doesn't, he will become hungry long before lunchtime and both his temper and concentration will be affected. A healthy mid-morning snack, for instance, a piece of fruit or cereal bar, will help tide him over until the next meal. If food is going to be provided for him, try to find out what will be on offer; provide him with a nutritious and healthy packed lunch if you are not happy or if there are no arrangements to feed him. Lunch need not always be sandwiches: try chicken pieces and potato salad, pieces of raw vegetables with a yoghurt dip, or other foods that your child can eat with his fingers.

Children are often encouraged to try new foods because they see their friends eat them, and you may find once your child starts at playgroup or school that he will want to eat foods that he previously rejected at home.

FAST FOODS

When you are out with your child and want to stop for a snack, do try not to resort too often to fast food restaurants: chips, hamburgers, sausages and soft drinks are high in salt, fats and sugar. If you can, take some healthy snack foods with you or choose somewhere that offers more healthy foods, for instance, sandwiches and salads. If your child particularly asks for hamburgers and chips, however, you may like to indulge him now and again – but make it clear that such foods are a special treat, to be eaten only now and then. My family used to eat at a hamburger restaurant once a week, for Saturday lunch. This satisfied everyone and is not so frequent as to damage good health.

EATING OUT

There will be many occasions when you will want to take your child out to eat. Being prepared will make the experience more enjoyable.

• *Try to find out beforehand what facilities are available at the restaurant you have chosen: if you are booking a table, tell them that you will be bringing young children, and find out whether there will be room for your child's pushchair and whether a high chair can be provided if you need one.*

• *Many children's menus are very limited and offer just hamburgers, sausages or fish fingers – all with chips. If you don't want your child to have these foods, ask whether you can order a small portion of a suitable dish from the main menu, and whether you will be charged full price for it.*

• *Most children will enjoy the experience of eating out, and you should involve your child fully, allowing him to choose his own meal and to give his own order to the waiter if he is not too shy.*

• *Take your child's booster seat with you if he normally uses one. If you think he will have difficulty drinking from a glass, you could also take along his trainer cup.*

• *Many restaurants positively encourage children and will be happy to provide straws for drinks, bibs and high chairs for young babies, and even small gifts such as paper hats or pictures to colour in.*

OVERWEIGHT

Obesity is one of the most common nutritional problems among children in prosperous Western societies. Most plump children, however, are not medically overweight and no special action is needed as long as they are healthy and active.

If you think that your child is overweight (that is, markedly fatter than his friends), consult your doctor who will know if your child's weight is above the normal range for his height.

The commonest causes of being overweight are lack of exercise and a poor diet. The best help for the child is often for the whole family to eat a healthier diet: less fat and sugar, more fresh fruit and vegetables and more unrefined carbohydrates.

Never aim to make your child lose weight but rather to keep his weight stable as he grows in height. Try these guidelines:

- *Bake, grill or boil foods rather than roasting or frying.*

- *Give water or diluted fruit juice, never sweetened drinks, when your child is thirsty.*

- *Give wholemeal bread, raw vegetables and fruit as snacks.*

- *Use wholemeal bread, pasta and rice instead of white kinds.*

- *Play lively games with your child to encourage activity.*

- *No child needs more than 500 ml (one pint) of milk a day. Skimmed or semi-skimmed cows' milk is fine for children over one year if vitamin supplements are also given.*

FEEDING PROBLEMS

Some young children are "difficult eaters", but in many cases the real difficulty is with a parent who expects the child to conform to an eating pattern that doesn't suit him. If you approach feeding problems with sympathy and a flexible attitude, they will usually just disappear. In some cases, there may be a genuine problem, such as intolerance to certain foodstuffs, or allergy (see p. 27), and you should then consult your doctor. Never attempt to determine and isolate a food allergy on your own.

FOOD PREFERENCES

In the second year, your child will start to show likes and dislikes for certain foods. It is very common for children to go through phases of eating only one kind of food and refusing everything else. For example, he may go for a week eating nothing but yoghurt and fruit, then suddenly go right off yoghurt and start eating nothing but cheese and mashed potato. Don't get cross with your child about this and don't insist that he eats certain foods. No single food is essential to your child and there is always a nutritious substitute for any food he refuses to eat. As long as you offer your child a wide variety of foods, he will be getting a balanced diet, and it is far better for him to eat something that he likes (even if it is something you do not approve of) than to eat nothing at all. The one thing you must watch out for is your toddler refusing to eat all foods from a particular group: refusing fruits or vegetables of any kind, for instance. If he does, his diet will become unbalanced, so you will have to think of ways of tempting him to eat fruit and vegetables, perhaps by cooking the food in a different way or by presenting it imaginatively (see pp. 35–93).

If you spend time and effort cooking food that you know your toddler doesn't want, you'll feel annoyed and resentful when he doesn't eat it, so give yourself and your child a break and make life easier on both of you by cooking food that you know he will enjoy.

Don't try to camouflage a disliked food by mixing it with something else, or bargain with your child by offering a favourite food if he eats the disliked one; he may very well end up refusing other foods as well. If you are introducing a new food, make sure your child is hungry; that way, he is more likely to accept it. Never try to force your child to

...ke something that he doesn't want; if he thinks it is very ...nportant to you, he will simply use the situation as a way ...f manipulating you to get what he wants.

REFUSAL TO EAT

...ot eating is an early indication that your child may be ...nwell or unhappy, so observe him carefully. If he looks ...ale and seems fretful and more clumsy than usual, check ...s temperature and speak to your doctor if you're worried.

Occasionally, your child may have eaten a lot of snacks ...r a drink of milk before his meal and he won't show his ...sual appetite. As long as the snacks are nutritious, this is ...othing to worry about. If he refuses to eat for no reason ...at you can see, don't let yourself be bothered by it. Your ...ild will always eat as much food as he really needs, and if ...ou insist on him eating, mealtimes may turn into a battle ...at you will always lose.

FOOD INTOLERANCE

...he inability to digest certain foods has to be distinguished ...om a true food allergy (see p. 27): this is quite different ...nd very rare. Intolerance occurs when the digestive system ...ils to produce essential enzymes that break down food ...side the body. Lactose intolerance – the inability to digest ...e sugars in cows' milk – is one of the most common ...orms of food intolerance in children. The enzyme (in this ...stance lactase) may be absent from birth or its production ...ay have been disrupted by an intestinal disorder, ...or example gastroenteritis. Gluten sensitivity, ...owever, is a true allergy (see p. 27) and causes ...flammation of the bowel. Smelly, ...ulky, pale stools are characteristic ...f the disorder, and you may notice ...at your child fails to gain weight ...nd appears listless. If he habitually ...as symptoms such as diarrhoea, ...ausea or pain after eating a ...ertain food, consult your doctor. ...he best remedy is just to avoid ...at food. You'll need expert ...edical advice to pin down the ...ulprit food and to rule out other ...ossible causes. Gluten sensitivity ...eeds careful medical supervision.

(see p. 27)

WHEN YOUR CHILD IS ILL

Loss of appetite is often one of the first signs of illness in a child, but this need not be a cause for concern if the illness lasts only a short time.

- *Your child must drink plenty of fluid, especially if he has been vomiting or has had diarrhoea.*

- *Most doctors recommend that drinks containing milk should be avoided if your child is suffering from gastroenteritis.*

- *There is no need for a special invalid diet, although it is sensible to avoid rich or heavy foods if your child has an upset stomach.*

- *Offer some of his favourite foods to cheer him up, and give smaller portions than usual. Because your child is resting, he will probably not want to eat very much.*

Good fluid intake
Although your child's appetite may be poor when she is ill, make sure she takes in plenty of fluid by offering her favourite drink.

NUTRITION

Given a free choice, your baby will always take enoug[h] food for his needs. If he doesn't want to eat, then he doesn['t] need to. This means that there will be days when he will ea[t] hardly anything, followed by periods of eating a lot.

To eat a balanced diet, your baby should eat foods fro[m] each one of the four different food groups, in roughly th[e] correct proportions (see below). This doesn't have to be o[n] a daily basis, however, so when you are considering wheth[er] he is eating well, you need to think in the long term: loo[k] at what he has eaten in the last week, not just in a singl[e] day. Viewed like this, a "binge" of eating nothing but brea[d] or potatoes for two days is nothing to worry about, sinc[e] your baby will probably take in enough fruit and vegetable[s] during the week to balance this out. What is important [is] that you should be giving him a wide variety of foods t[o] choose from: he can't eat the foods he requires if they a[re] not made available to him.

Your baby will gradually come to eat many of the sam[e] foods as you, prepared in a form that he can manage. [It] would be wrong, however, to suppose that his needs are th[e] same as yours, or that a diet that would be recommende[d] as healthy for you will be good for him. You may aim t[o] reduce your fat intake by using low-fat dairy products, fo[r] example, but you should give your child whole milk unt[il]

The food pyramid
This table identifies the proportions in which the main food groups should be eaten in order for your baby to take in the right balance of nutrients. Carbohydrates and fruit and vegetables are the two most important groups; protein-rich foods such as meat, fish, eggs, dairy produce, nuts and pulses come next. Fats, oils and sugars should form the smallest part of your baby's diet – in fact, the amounts of these that occur naturally in other foods will be more than enough to meet his needs. By following these guidelines for your baby, you will be helping him form good habits for life.

FATS, OILS AND SUGARS

PROTEINS: MEAT, FISH, EGGS, DAIRY PRODUCE, NUTS AND PULSES

FIBRE AND VITAMINS: FRUIT AND VEGETABLES

CARBOHYDRATES: BREAD, CEREALS, RICE AND PASTA

e is two years old, unless he is overweight (see p. 24); after that, you can introduce semi-skimmed milk if you wish. The health benefits of limiting sugar intake, however, apply just as much to babies as to adults. Never add salt to your baby's food: his kidneys are too immature to cope with it.

FOOD ALLERGY

Most cases of suspected food allergy turn out to be no more than intolerance (see p. 25) or the combination of a fussy child and a fussy mother. A true food allergy is quite rare, and occurs when the the body's immune system undergoes an exaggerated reaction to a protein or chemical that it interprets as "foreign". Allergy is a protective mechanism of the body, and symptoms can include headache, nausea, profuse vomiting, a rash, widespread red blotches in the skin and swelling of the mouth, tongue, face and eyes. The likelihood of your child suffering an allergic reaction is greater if there is a history of allergies in the family.

At first the allergen – which is the substance that causes the reaction – may produce only mild symptoms, but these may become more severe if the child is repeatedly exposed to the food concerned. If you introduce new foods one at a time, with one-week intervals between each introduction, you'll easily recognize any symptoms and be able to consult your doctor. Certain foods like wheat (gluten sensitivity, see p. 25) and egg whites are more likely to cause problems and should be introduced after six months of age. Shellfish, strawberries, nuts, chocolate and cows' milk also cause allergic reactions. There has been much publicity about sensitivity to food colourings and flavourings as well. In fact, very few children react in an abnormal way as a result of these food additives, but avoid them if you can.

More recent studies have cast doubt on previous claims that food allergies are the cause of behavioural disturbances (including hyperactivity) in children: parents continued to report behavioural disturbance even when the suspect food had been withdrawn from the child's diet, unknown to them. In a very small number of cases, it has been proved that food was responsible for the behaviour, but in very many more cases bad behaviour is a way of seeking love and attention from neglectful parents. You should never try to isolate a food allergy on your own without expert medical advice and never assume an allergy is present without a clear diagnosis from a paediatric allergist.

FOODS TO AVOID

For safety, you should avoid giving foods that are easy to choke on – that is, small, hard and easy to swallow, such as peanuts – until your child is 2–3 years old and able to chew well. Other foods that may not be directly harmful to your child but are best limited because they offer very little nutritional value are listed below:

- *Highly sweetened foods (jams, commercial desserts, sweetened condensed milk, biscuits, cakes and all sweets).*

- *Processed meats (salami, bacon, ham, meat pies and cured and cooked sausages).*

- *Saturated fats (cream).*

- *Canned foods with added salt or sugar (check all labels).*

- *Syrup drinks and squashes.*

- *Salty foods like crisps and foods containing hidden salt, such as stock cubes.*

A BALANCED DIET

As your child grows, his nutritional requirements increase proportionately: greater quantities of certain nutrients are needed during growth spurts and when he is learning to walk. Your child's diet should contain sufficient amounts of protein, carbohydrates, fats, vitamins and minerals, and he will get all of these as long as you provide a wide variety of foods. Because he is growing, he still needs more protein and calories for his body weight than an adult.

Broadly speaking, eating a variety of foods from three of the four food groups – carbohydrates, fruit and vegetables (fibre) and protein-rich foods (see p. 26) – will fulfil your child's needs. However, some foods within the groups have particular nutritional value. All fruits and vegetables provide carbohydrates and fibre, for instance, and leafy vegetables such as cabbage are especially high in minerals, while citrus fruits are a good source of vitamins A and C (see chart).

A good diet is a varied one
Variety is the key to a balanced diet. Choose foods from each of the groups in the chart.

NUTRIENTS FOUND IN DIFFERENT KINDS OF FOODS

FOODS	CONSISTING OF	NUTRIENTS SUPPLIED
BREADS AND CEREALS	Wholemeal bread, noodles, pasta, rice	Protein, carbohydrates, B group vitamins, iron, calcium
CITRUS FRUITS	Oranges, grapefruits, lemons, limes, tangerines	Vitamins A and C
FATS	Butter, margarine, vegetable oils, fish oils, nut oils	Vitamins A and D, essential fatty acids
GREEN AND YELLOW VEGETABLES	Cabbage, sprouts, spinach, kale, green beans, squash, lettuce, celery, courgettes	Minerals, including calcium, chlorine, fluorine, chromium, cobalt, copper, zinc, manganese, potassium, sodium, magnesium
OTHER VEGETABLES AND FRUITS	Potatoes, beetroot, corn, carrots, cauliflower, pineapples, apricots, nectarines, peaches, strawberries, plums, apples, bananas	Carbohydrates, vitamins A and C, B group vitamins
HIGH PROTEIN FOODS	Chicken, fish, lamb, beef, pork, offal, eggs, cheese, nuts, legumes	Protein, fat, iron, vitamins A and D, B group vitamins especially B^{12} (naturally present in animal proteins only)
MILK AND DAIRY PRODUCTS	Milk, cream, yoghurt, fromage frais, ice cream, cheese	Protein, fat, calcium, vitamins A and D, B group vitamins

SNACKS

Until the age of four or five, your child will prefer to eat often throughout the day. His stomach still cannot cope with three adult-sized meals a day, so he is not ready for an adult eating pattern. Typically, he will want to eat five to seven times a day. What he eats is more important than how often he eats. As a rule, the more meals he has, the smaller they will be.

You may be accustomed to thinking of snacks as "extras", but they're an integral part of any child's diet so should not be refused. As long as the snacks do not reduce your child's daily nutrition and are not used as substitutes for "meals", snacks can be wonderfully useful for introducing new foods gradually without disrupting your child's eating patterns. Avoid giving your child highly refined and processed foods like biscuits, sweets, cakes and ice cream, which contain a lot of calories and very few nutrients. Fresh vegetables and fruits, cubes of cheese, cheese sandwiches with wholemeal bread and fruit juice all make good, nutritious snacks.

How to plan snacks Snack foods should contribute to the whole day's nutrition, so don't leave them to chance: plan them carefully and co-ordinate meals and snacks so that you serve different foods in the snacks and in the meals.

• Milk and milk-based drinks make very good snacks and contain protein, calcium and many of the B group vitamins. You should use whole milk until your child is at least two years old; then you can use semi-skimmed but not skimmed milk unless your child is overweight (see p. 24). Raw fruit juices are also very nutritious and have a lot of vitamin C. If you buy fruit juice drinks, avoid those with added sugar.

• Your child may become bored with certain kinds of food, so try to give him lots of variety and make snacks amusing and decorative if you can (see pp. 77–84).

Food that your child rejects in one form may be acceptable to him in another, for instance, yoghurt can be frozen so that it becomes more like ice cream. A child who rejects cheese sandwiches might enjoy eating cubes or slices of cheese and tomato pieces out of an ice-cream cone.

• You can also increase your child's interest in food by involving him in planning – or even preparing – part of a snack. He will take great pride in eating a sandwich if he has helped you wash or tear the lettuce, for example, or if you allow him to assemble the bread and filling himself.

Little and often
Your child will need more snacks than you do, since he isn't able to eat large meals.

KITCHEN HYGIENE

Scares about food-poisoning in recent years have made parents much more conscious of the dangers of poor food hygiene. The commonsense precautions given here will protect your baby.

- *Always wash your hands with soap before handling food, especially after using the toilet or changing a nappy and after playing with pets. Make sure your family does the same.*

- *Be scrupulous about keeping the kitchen clean, especially work surfaces, chopping boards and utensils used in food preparation. Never use wooden utensils: they harbour millions of germs.*

- *Always use a clean tea-towel or paper towels to dry dishes, or let them dry in a rack after rinsing them with hot water.*

- *Keep the kitchen waste-bin covered and empty it often. Rinse out the bin with hot water and a little disinfectant every time you empty it.*

- *Cover any food that is left out of the cupboard.*

- *Throw away any food that is left over in your baby's bowl.*

FOOD PREPARATION

Once your baby is on solids, it is no longer necessary to sterilize all feeding utensils, although bottles and teats used for milk should still be sterilized until your baby is about nine months old. Cups, bowls and cutlery can be washed in hot, soapy water and rinsed with hot water; let them dry in a rack or use a clean tea-towel or paper towels. Now that your baby's diet includes a range of foods, however, you need to take sensible precautions to protect him from the effects of harmful bacteria such as salmonella and listeria poisoning, so you should be well informed about buying, storing, cooking, reheating and preparing food safely.

BUYING AND STORING

The most important thing to look for when buying food is freshness. Shop often, and use food as quickly as possible. Bruised or damaged fruits and vegetables deteriorate rapidly so don't buy them. Always wash fruits if the skin is to be eaten, since there may be a residue of insecticides or other chemicals on it. Most processed foods now carry a "sell by" or "best before" date, so check this and make sure that there are no signs of damage to packets, cans or jars.

Food that is stored in the refrigerator should be in clean covered containers. Store cooked and raw foods on separate shelves and put raw meat and fish on plates or in dishes, or their juices could drip onto foods on the shelf below. Check the package to see that the food is suitable for freezing, and never freeze foods for longer than the time recommended by the manufacturer: this will depend on the star rating of your freezer. Always defrost frozen foods thoroughly before using, and never refreeze food once it has been defrosted.

COOKING AND REHEATING

Always cook your baby's food very thoroughly; this applies especially to meat, poultry and eggs. Never give your baby raw or soft-cooked eggs, liver pâté, soft cheeses such as Brie or Camembert or cheeses made with unpasteurized milk. It is best not to give your baby reheated leftovers or foods that have been refrozen. If you're preparing food in bulk quantities, don't leave it to cool before putting it into the refrigerator because this will just give the bacteria a chance to multiply. Put the food in cold containers, cover it tightly and put it straight into the refrigerator or freezer.

PREPARING

At first, you'll have to purée all of your baby's food, but this stage won't last very long, so if you don't have a blender or liquidizer, it's probably best just to get an inexpensive hand-operated food-mill. A nylon sieve will be perfectly adequate to begin with. As your baby gets older, you can feed him coarser foods. By the time he is six months old, he will be able to manage a thicker purée, and at nine months he can enjoy a mash with small chunks of meat or vegetables in it.

You can use a variety of different liquids to thin down home-prepared foods: the water you've used to steam fruits or vegetables is ideal because it contains valuable nutrients. To thicken foods, you can use ground, wholegrain cereals such as wheatgerm, or cottage cheese, yoghurt or mashed potato. If you feel you need to sweeten foods, use naturally sweet fruit juice or dextrose rather than refined sugar.

TIPS FOR PREPARING FOODS SAFELY

Do…	Don't…
• use fruits and vegetables as soon as possible after buying • peel tough-skinned fruits and vegetables if the skin is likely to cause your baby problems • cook soft-skinned fruits and vegetables in their skins: this helps to retain their vitamins and provides additional fibre • cook fruits and vegetables in a steamer or in a tightly covered pan with as little water as possible. This helps to retain the vitamins that are normally lost in cooking • give your baby cooked and puréed meat or fish. The purée can be thinned with vegetable water or soup • use sunflower or corn oil. Never cook with butter or other saturated fats	• buy bruised or wrinkled fruits and vegetables • leave prepared vegetables to soak in water, since this destroys their vitamins • slice or cut up fruits and vegetables a long time in advance, since vitamin content will be lost • give red meat more than twice a week, since it has a high saturated fat content • overcook or boil tinned foods, since this destroys their vitamins • add salt or sugar to your child's food: his immature kidneys can't handle a great deal of salt, and giving him sweet foods at an early age will encourage a sweet tooth • leave prepared foods to cool at room temperature: refrigerate them right away

PROCESSED FOODS

Processed foods are more expensive than ones you make yourself at home, but they are convenient, especially if you are in a hurry or travelling. Always observe the following guidelines when using them.

• *Check the ingredients; they are listed in order of quantity, with the greatest amount first. Anything that has water near the top of the list will not be very nutritious.*

• *Avoid all foods with added sugar or modified starch. It is illegal for baby foods to contain added salt or monosodium glutamate (MSG).*

• *Make sure that any seal is intact: if it is damaged, the food could be contaminated.*

• *Don't heat up the food in the jar: the glass might crack.*

• *Don't feed your baby from the jar if you intend to keep some of the food, because the leftovers will be contaminated with saliva. You can feed your baby from the jar if he's likely to eat the whole lot.*

• *Don't keep opened jars in the refrigerator for longer than two days and never beyond the "best before" or "sell by" date.*

• *Never store food in an opened tin: transfer it to a dish, cover and refrigerate.*

• *Check the ingredients lists carefully if you are introducing food types gradually. Many processed foods contain eggs, gluten and dairy products.*

FRUITS AND VEGETABLES

Fresh fruits and vegetables are best; frozen are second bes
If you use canned varieties, make sure to check the labels s
you can avoid those with additives and extra salt and suga

Fresh vegetables are rich in nutrients, colours, flavou
and textures. Wash leaf vegetables, and scrub root vegetabl
rather than peeling, if possible, since most nutrients lie ju
beneath the skin. Cook for the least amount of time as soo

FACTS ABOUT FRESH VEGETABLES AND HOW TO USE THEM

Type	How to Use
Asparagus	Good in soups, quiches, salads. Simmer for 10 minutes. Serve only the tips.
Aubergines	Always peel. Baked and puréed it has a good creamy texture, especially good when mixed with a small quantity of mayonnaise
Avocados	Always peel. Good texture for babies. A rich source of unsaturated fat.
Beansprouts	Easily digested and full of nutrients. Good snack food. You can sprout pulses such as alfalfa or mung beans to make your own beansprouts at home.
Beetroot	Always peel. Good in soups, sandwiches, salads and drinks. May turn urine red, so don't be alarmed.
Broad beans	Serve when young and pale green. Good in soups, casseroles and sauces.
Broccoli	Rich in vitamin C. Good in soups and quiches. Avoid any with yellow tips.
Brussels sprouts	Choose young, small ones. Simmer lightly or steam. Can be served as a finger food with cheese sauce.
Cabbage	Stuff the leaves or use in soups and stews. Finely grate for salads.
Carrots	Rich in vitamin A. Sweet, colourful all-rounder. Use in drinks and for baking.
Cauliflower	Use unblemished florets. Easy to digest. Good in soups, sauces and salads.
Celeriac	Stores well. Peel. Lemon juice stops discoloration. Good in soups and salads.
Celery	Remove stringy parts for babies. Stuff with soft cheese or purées. Use leaves too.
Chinese cabbage	Also known as Chinese leaves, pak choi or bok choy. Mild, slightly sweet flavour. Good stir-fried.
Courgettes	Steam and mix with pieces of tomato for a quick meal.
Cucumber	Always peel. Stuff with cheese. Grate into yoghurt for a quick sauce.
Garlic	An acquired taste. Always peel. Use sparingly in cooked dishes.
Green beans	Tender dwarf beans are best. Frozen are a useful standby.

s they are prepared. Baking, braising, stir-frying, steaming
nd boiling are good methods; try to use any cooking juices
r water in stocks, soups and sauces. You may like to blanch
egetables such as cauliflower to make them less hard when
rving them as finger foods to children under 12 months.

Check fruits for ripeness, wash well and ideally peel them
ntil your child is about 18 months old (then he should get
sed to chewing any thin peel, since it is a good source of
bre). Remove stones or pips until he's about two years old.

FACTS ABOUT FRESH VEGETABLES AND HOW TO USE THEM

TYPE	HOW TO USE
LEEKS	Always peel. Steam, braise or stir-fry. Good in soups or any vegetable dish.
LETTUCE	Many colourful varieties. Shred or use leaf as a container for other foods.
MANGETOUT	Also known as snow peas. Eat whole or stuff. Serve with lemon juice.
MUSHROOMS	Peel. Cook larger ones. Stuff with rice or cheese. Use small ones in salads.
OLIVES	Rather salty, but many children love them. Green are milder than black.
ONIONS	Always peel. Mince and use sparingly. Try milder varieties such as red onions.
PARSLEY	Rich in vitamins, iron and minerals. Good as a garnish and in sauces.
PARSNIPS	Sweet flavour. Peel. Mash with carrots or potatoes. Purée or slice with meats.
PEAS	Use small tender peas. Purée for a bright green dip. Frozen are a good standby.
PEPPERS	Steam or grill in skins and peel. Red, yellow and orange tend to be sweeter, green are rich in vitamin C.
POTATOES	Cook in skins to retain nutrients. Purée with carrots, beetroot or peas.
PUMPKIN	Always peel. Bake, steam or sauté. Purée with cheese. Also good in pies.
SPINACH	Rich in minerals. Serve tender young leaves raw. Wash well. Cooks quickly in water clinging to leaves after washing. Good mixed with soft cheese.
SQUASH	Peel. Easily puréed. Good sautéed with cheese or herbs, or stuffed and baked.
SWEDE	Always peel. Boil and mash with yoghurt. Use in soups or any savoury dish.
SWEETCORN	Cook thoroughly. Hard for babies to digest.
TOMATOES	Very versatile and rich in vitamin C. Good stuffed, either raw or baked.
TURNIPS	Always peel. Takes on other flavours well when cooked. Season with herbs.
WATERCRESS	Good source of vitamins and minerals. Use in soups, salads, sandwiches.
YAMS	Peel. Also known as sweet potato. Boil or bake. Good mashed with yoghurt.

FACTS ABOUT FRESH FRUITS AND HOW TO USE THEM

TYPE	HOW TO USE
APPLES	Good all-rounder and as an instant snack. Purée and add to yoghurt. Bake in skins, stuffed with dried fruits.
APRICOTS	Fresh or dried. Source of vitamin A. Serve fresh ones ripe, peeled and sliced.
BANANAS	A good first fruit. Easy to mash and mix with other foods. Good with cereals.
BLACKBERRIES	Must be ripe. Cook to a purée for juice, which stains. Good with other fruits.
CHERRIES	Must be ripe. Juice stains so supervise eating.
CURRANTS	Must be ripe. Cook and purée for babies. Use sparingly: can be sharp to taste.
DATES	Fresh or dried. Remove stones and stuff with cheese.
DRIED FRUITS	Rich in minerals. Wash and soak to soften. Serve as snacks, desserts or as sweeteners mixed with other fruits.
FIGS	Fresh or dried. Good mixed with yoghurt. Chop up for snacks.
GRAPES	Choose seedless varieties. Peel if child cannot chew skin.
GRAPEFRUITS	Choose ripe ones. Remove all pith; never add sugar. Pink varieties are sweeter.
KIWI FRUITS	Rich in vitamin C and an attractive colour.
LEMONS	Use juice and finely grated peel in cooking and drinks. Juice prevents other raw fruits from discolouring.
MANGOES	Sweet and juicy. A source of vitamin A. Purée with milk for fruit dessert.
MELONS	Many varieties. Ripe pieces are refreshing and have soft flesh.
ORANGES	Like all citrus fruits, a juicy source of vitamin C. Cut off all pith for babies.
PAPAYAS	Also known as pawpaw. Soft, juicy texture. Good for breakfast and in salads.
PEACHES/ NECTARINES	Peaches have skins with fuzzy texture; nectarines have smooth skins. Poach or serve raw if very ripe. Use halved as a container for fruit salads.
PEARS	Good raw or baked. Also good with cubes of cheese for snacks.
PINEAPPLE	Remove core and use for teething. Juicy, fibrous fruit.
PLUMS	Many varieties. Serve very ripe ones raw, or stew in a little water with orange juice instead of sugar. Purée makes a good "jam".
PRUNES	Soak to remove stones. Stew and serve with yoghurt. Purée to make a "jam".
RASPBERRIES	Good cooked or raw when ripe. Use to flavour cakes and yoghurt.
RHUBARB	Stew or bake with orange rind and juice or dried fruits instead of sugar.
STRAWBERRIES	Must be ripe. Introduce at around 12 months of age. Good in tarts or chopped and mixed with fromage frais.

EVERYDAY MEALS

There is no question that a child's diet is important because first foods and tastes – which your child will be trying out in her everyday meals and snacks – form the building blocks for her future diet and health.

Here, I've set out to inspire you with some wonderful shapes and ideas based on finger foods for children aged from nine months. Each meal is nutritionally balanced and in most cases can be adapted from the foods you choose and prepare for the rest of the family. You may have to make some changes in your cooking habits, but as a result you will probably all eat more healthily.

RECIPE HINTS AND TIPS

The recipes for the meals featured in this book are simple and flexible. The meals focus on eggs and cheese, or fish, or meat or vegetables, and there are also ideas for healthy snacks and food for special occasions.

Ingredients Don't hesitate to use alternative ingredients that will accommodate your child's preferences, or to use a food processor or blender to speed up preparation time. Where a recipe calls for flour, oil or sugar, try to use wholemeal flour, polyunsaturated vegetable oils, and raw brown sugar, which has a stronger flavour than white refined sugar, so you can use less to sweeten cakes and biscuits. Honey isn't used in the recipes. It is just another form of sugar, and it is wise not to give it to children under 12 months since it may contain harmful bacteria.

If you want to use salt in a dish for all the family, add it after removing your child's portion. This way, you will be encouraging a taste for real food rather than a taste for salt. Add herbs and spices for flavour instead.

Storage If a recipe makes more than you need, you can store the surplus in a covered, airtight container in the refrigerator; use within two days. Alternatively, you can freeze food, closely wrapped, for up to one month.

Stainless-steel grater

Hand-held blender

Preparing first foods
While your baby is getting used to solids, you will need to grate or purée vegetables for her. Steaming is a fast cooking method that helps to preserve all the nutrients.

Grated carrot

Collapsible steamer fits any pan

BREAKFAST

CEREALS

WHITE RICE

BROWN RICE

POT BARLEY

COMMERCIAL BABY RICE

BULGAR WHEAT

We should all eat more whole grain cereals and by including them in your child's diet from early on, you may come to eat more yourself. For most babies, their first solid food is an iron-rich commercial baby cereal. However, you can make your own mixes and grind them in a blender to get a finer texture. Use rice, oats, barley, rye, millet and wheat. Later, add dried or fresh fruits and ground nuts, and serve the cereal combined with milk, yoghurt or diluted apple juice. With ready-to-eat brands, read the labels carefully. Few are free of added salt and sugar, but you should be able to find unsweetened, salt-free brands if you shop around. Don't limit cereals to breakfast time. Use them as a topping, a thickener, a coating and when you bake, and don't forget the less usual varieties such as cornmeal and bulgar wheat.

COMMERCIAL CEREAL

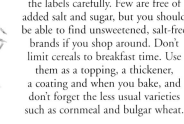

MILLET

GROUND MUESLI

CORNMEAL

SEMOLINA

ROLLED OATS

37

BREADS

PUMPERNICKEL
RYE BREAD

GRANARY
BREAD

FRENCH
BREAD

Wholemeal bread is the best
to serve your child but many other
high-fibre, whole grain breads are
available (the grains in granary bread
may be too tough for young babies).
If your child eats these most of the time,
the occasional slice of white bread is fine.
Always read the label carefully when
buying packaged bread. Some brown
breads are not wholemeal at all and
contain colouring. If you bake your own
bread, try to use 100 percent wholemeal
flour and experiment with adding
wheatgerm, sesame seeds and bran for
extra flavour. You can make any bread
look attractive by cutting it into shapes
using small biscuit cutters and serving it
with different spreads.

SODA BREAD

LIGHT RYE BREAD
WITH CARAWAY SEEDS

WHOLEWHEAT
BREAD
(recipe p. 41)

CORNBREAD
(recipe p. 41)

FRUIT BREAD

BLACK RYE BREAD

TELL-THE-TIME BREAKFAST

Bread, egg, soft cheese and fruit combine in a clock shape to form this breakfast. Older children will enjoy eating their way around the clock as they try to tell the time, and younger ones will simply like its shape. The bread pieces are dipped in beaten egg with a spoonful of milk added. After immersing the bread to get it thoroughly coated, fry it quickly in a non-stick frying pan brushed with a little oil. For a quicker meal, simply spread pieces of wholewheat bread with a fruity jam, fruit purée such as prune, or soft cheese and chopped fruit. Fruit is a good instant food, even at breakfast time, and you should try to serve a few slices of fresh fruit every day, as snacks and with meals.

Breakfast clock face with wholewheat bread
Dip eight bread pieces in egg and milk and fry. Spread four pieces with ricotta cheese and diced dried apricots. Arrange in a clock face and add banana for the hands. *(Recipe p. 41)*

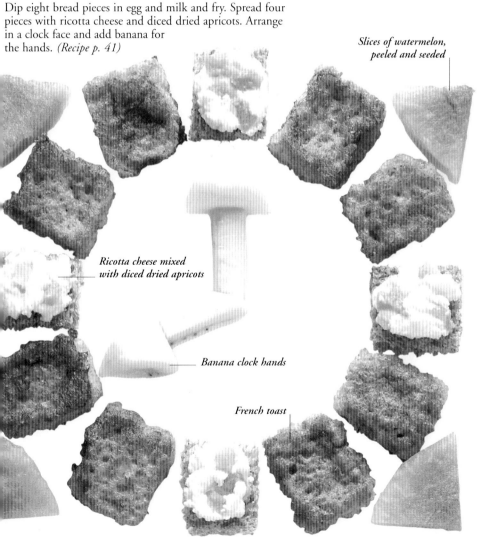

Slices of watermelon, peeled and seeded

Ricotta cheese mixed with diced dried apricots

Banana clock hands

French toast

SUNSHINE BREAKFAST

Every household has its own idea of what the traditional breakfast should be, but with young children, who are usually ravenous as soon as they wake up in the mornings, speed is of the essence. This cheery breakfast makes a change from the usual cereal and need not take long to prepare. Adding dried fruits to the drop scone gives it extra vitamins, fibre and iron. Serve it with oat biscuits and fresh orange segments, which are juicy and full of vitamin C (you may want to cut the pieces in half for younger children). Drop scones can be made in batches and then frozen. To serve, just defrost at room temperature and toast them lightly so they heat through.

Juicy fresh orange segments
Remove all the peel, pith and pips so that there is no risk of choking. Arrange the segments to look like the rays of the sun.

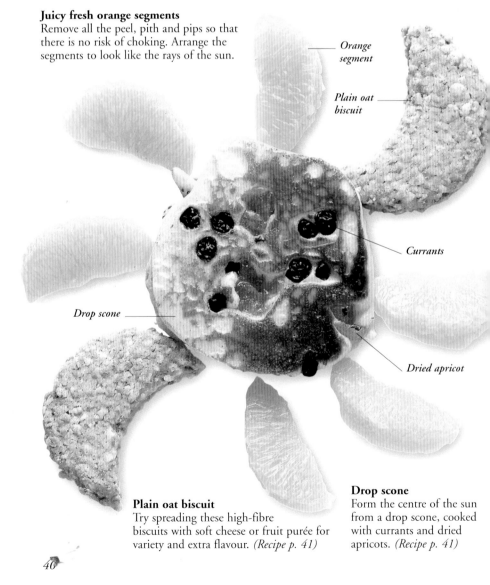

Orange segment

Plain oat biscuit

Currants

Drop scone

Dried apricot

Plain oat biscuit
Try spreading these high-fibre biscuits with soft cheese or fruit purée for variety and extra flavour. *(Recipe p. 41)*

Drop scone
Form the centre of the sun from a drop scone, cooked with currants and dried apricots. *(Recipe p. 41)*

BREAKFAST RECIPES

CORNBREAD *(page 38)*

Ingredients for 1 large cornbread
275 g (10 oz) self-raising flour
100 g (4 oz) sugar
2 tbsp baking powder
pinch of salt
225 g (8 oz) yellow cornmeal
4 eggs, beaten
600 ml (1 pint) milk
100 g (4 oz) butter or margarine, melted

1 Preheat oven to 200°C (400°F) Gas 6.
2 Mix all the dry ingredients together.
3 Add the lightly beaten eggs, milk and butter and mix for 1 minute until smooth.
4 Grease a 30 x 23 cm (12 x 9 in) baking tin and pour in the mixture.
5 Bake for 35 minutes. Cut into squares and serve warm.

WHOLEWHEAT BREAD *(page 39)*

Ingredients for 1 small loaf
350 g (12 oz) wholewheat flour
210 ml (⅓ pint) water
3 g (½ sachet) quick-acting dry yeast
1 dessertspoon vegetable oil
pinch of salt

1 Preheat oven to 230°C (450°F) Gas 8.
2 Place all the ingredients in a mixing bowl and mix together to form a dough.
3 Turn the dough onto a board and knead vigorously for 5 minutes.
4 Place the dough in a clean mixing bowl, cover and leave in a warm place to rise.
5 When the dough has doubled in size, form it into rolls and place on a greased baking tray. Alternatively, form it into a loaf shape and place in a greased 500 g (1 lb) loaf tin.
6 Bake rolls for 15–20 minutes, a loaf for 25–35 minutes or until the bread sounds hollow when tapped on the base.
7 Transfer rolls or turn out loaf onto a wire rack to cool thoroughly.

DROP SCONES *(page 40)*

Ingredients for about 15 drop scones
100 g (4 oz) flour
1 tsp bicarbonate of soda
1½ tsp cream of tartar
1 egg
150 ml (5 fl oz) milk
handful of dried fruits such as currants and apricots

1 Sieve the dry ingredients into a bowl.
2 Make a well in the centre, crack in the egg and add the milk. Mix to a batter.
3 Heat a small, non-stick frying pan and brush with a little oil. Drop a spoonful of the mixture onto the hot surface.
4 Sprinkle dried fruit onto the batter and turn over when bubbles appear on the surface (after 1 or 2 minutes). Cook for a minute or two to brown the other side.
5 Repeat with rest of mixture. Keep scones warm by wrapping them in a clean cloth.
6 To freeze, cool and store in a container between layers of greaseproof paper.

PLAIN OAT BISCUITS *(page 40)*

Ingredients for about 20 biscuits
50 g (2 oz) flour
175 g (6 oz) oatmeal
50 g (2 oz) rolled oats
pinch of bicarbonate of soda
100 g (4 oz) butter or margarine
1 egg yolk

1 Preheat oven to 180°C (350°F) Gas 4.
2 Mix all the dry ingredients together.
3 Rub in the fat until the mixture resembles fine breadcrumbs.
4 Mix to a firm dough with the egg yolk.
5 Turn onto a board and knead lightly. Roll out to a thickness of 6 mm (¼ in).
6 Cut into shapes with biscuit cutters or a knife and transfer to a greased baking tray.
7 Bake the biscuits for about 15 minutes or until they are lightly browned.

EGG AND CHEESE MEALS

EGG SAIL-BOATS

Although eggs are a good source of protein and iron, you should introduce them into your child's diet gradually – first the yolk, then the white when she is 10–12 months old. Check for any reaction or allergy (see p. 27) and use sparingly. Three or four eggs a week is about right for young children, so if you use eggs a lot in cooking, offer slices rather than halves when serving these sail-boats. Add a portion of wholemeal bread and a brightly coloured, tempting vegetable. Mangetout (snow peas), here stuffed with mashed cottage cheese, are tender and fun to eat. Alternatively, fill crisp lettuce hearts or lightly steamed or raw celery sticks with the fibrous strands removed.

Gouda cheese

Bread fish
Serve wholemeal bread cut into jolly shapes.

Hard-boiled egg

Cottage cheese

Cooked pea

Mangetout (snow pea)

Green pea boat
Steam mangetout and fill with mashed cottage cheese. Decorate each boat with a few cooked green peas.

Chewy apricot slices
Spread puréed apricots on a baking tray and bake in the oven at its lowest setting for 8 hours. Cool and store in the refrigerator.

Egg sail-boats
Hard boil an egg and cut it in half. Cut triangles from a slice of Gouda cheese for the sails. Make an incision in the egg halves to secure the sails.

Apricot slice

CAT AND MOUSE

If your child has been introduced to a cat, or a story about a cat and a mouse, she will find these shapes particularly interesting. The cat's face is a simple one-egg omelette with diced boiled potato and fresh parsley added to it. Parsley is rich in calcium, iron and vitamins. Serve it finely chopped as an edible garnish to add colour to any meal.

Fill the omelette with whatever vegetables you have to hand so that it holds its shape. Add extra flavour and texture with herbs, grated cheese or crunchy beansprouts. Cut the omelette into strips and reassemble the shape before adding the lettuce, carrot and celery features so that your child can pick up and eat the pieces as finger food.

Cat-face omelette
Make the cat's features from lettuce leaves, pieces of cooked carrot and steamed celery strips, and its face from a one-egg omelette, flecked with parsley and containing diced cooked potato. *(Recipe p. 48)*

Sultana nose

Peeled, seedless grape halves

Crisp lettuce heart ears

— *Strip of fresh pear*

Pear mouse
Peel a ripe pear, cut it in half and core. Peel a seedless grape, cut it in half and secure in slits for the ears. Use a strip of pear for the mouse's tail and add a soaked sultana for its nose.

Omelette

Carrot nose and eyes

Sliced celery whiskers

CHEESY MONSTER

This friendly monster is easily made from a simple, tasty cheese and lentil bake, cut into shapes and decorated with a realistic spiny back, forked tail and sturdy legs. Lentils are economical, quick to cook and extremely nutritious, whether you choose red, brown or green varieties. They mix well with any cooked vegetable and make a protein-rich meal when prepared in combination with cheese, egg and wholemeal breadcrumbs or wheatgerm. The dip-style dessert is a blend of Quark, fromage frais or any other low-fat soft cheese and raspberry purée (you may need to sieve the purée to get rid of pips). The mixture is perfect for sucking off pieces of fresh fruit, biscuits or even fingers.

Cheesy monster
The cheese and lentil bake that forms the monster can be served hot or cold. Soft steamed courgette provides a nice contrast of texture. *(Recipe p. 48)*

Sliced green olive

Squeeze of tomato purée

Raspberry dip
Purée ripe or lightly cooked raspberries without sugar. Mix with the same amount of Quark or another low-fat soft cheese and serve the dip with fresh fruit or biscuits.

Cheese and l bake forms body and he

Peeled raw apple

MAKING THE MOST OF CHEESE

Cheese in any form is an excellent food for children, but don't rely only on traditional hard, high-fat cheeses like Cheddar. Try medium-fat cheeses such as Edam, Gouda and Swiss and Scandinavian varieties like Emmenthal or Jarlsberg. These are mild in flavour and many have holes, which are interesting to children. Don't hesitate to introduce soft French cheeses, made from pasteurized milk; Camembert and Brie are often favourites because of their creamy texture and mild flavour. Remove the rind before serving. Low-fat soft cheeses such as cottage cheese, Quark, ricotta, fromage frais and curd cheese are easy to digest and can be added to dishes in place of milk.

Soft steamed courgette

EDAM AS A
RABBIT

LOW-FAT SOFT CHEESE
AS A BUTTERFLY

GRILLED BRIE AS A STAR

JARLSBERG
AS A GIRAFFE

CHEESE ON TOAST
AS A PENGUIN

RICOTTA AND CHOPPED
APRICOTS AS A HEART

Exciting cheese shapes
Cutting hard or firm cheese into shapes with miniature biscuit cutters will add to its appeal for your child.

SMILEY FACE PIZZA

Pizza is a favourite meal for all the family and can be prepared in individual portions to suit your child. You can make it with a traditional yeast dough or a simple scone dough, as here, for ease and quickness. For extra speed, use a halved muffin or a slice of pitta bread as a base. Lightly toast one side, put some grated cheese on the other, spread on the topping, decorate and grill until the cheese melts. The basic pizza topping of tomatoes, chopped onions and cheese can be livened up for the rest of the family with tuna fish, anchovies or olives. Keep your child's portion lighter in flavour and allow it to cool well before serving: cheese retains its heat and can easily scald a young mouth.

Smiley face pizza
This all-in-one meal consists of a scone-based pizza decorated with cheese, vegetables and pieces of fresh fruit.
(Recipe p. 48)

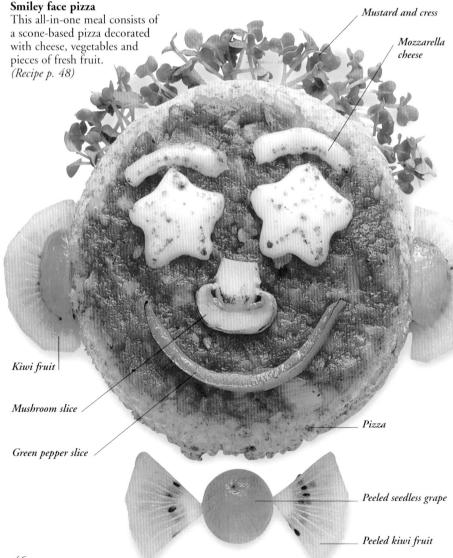

Mustard and cress

Mozzarella cheese

Kiwi fruit

Mushroom slice

Green pepper slice

Pizza

Peeled seedless grape

Peeled kiwi fruit

QUICHE FLOWER

Most adults were brought up to believe that the savoury part of any meal ought to be eaten first, but by serving savoury and sweet foods together, you are offering your child a wider choice in flavours. There is no harm in starting off a meal with something sweet, such as these slices of mango or any other pieces of fresh fruit. But avoid letting your child fill up on sugary and fattening sweets, cakes, biscuits and desserts. Try to liven up dishes that would otherwise look plain by adding brightly coloured edible garnishes: the watercress used here is rich in vitamin A and many minerals. This wholesome meal gets an extra boost to its nutritional value in a cup of naturally sweet carrot juice.

Quiche flower
For a complete meal, serve fresh fruit alongside a vegetable quiche made with wholemeal pastry. *(Recipe p. 48)*

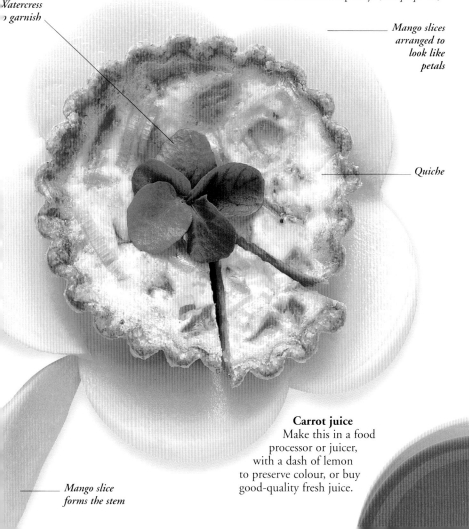

Watercress
garnish

Mango slices
arranged to
look like
petals

Quiche

Carrot juice
Make this in a food
processor or juicer,
with a dash of lemon
to preserve colour, or buy
good-quality fresh juice.

Mango slice
forms the stem

EGG AND CHEESE RECIPES

CAT FACE OMELETTE *(page 43)*

Ingredients for 1 serving
 1 egg
 15 ml (1 tbsp) water
 1 tbsp finely chopped parsley (and other
  herbs such as chives, optional)
 1 small boiled potato, diced (and other
  vegetables such as beansprouts, optional)
 small knob of butter
 1 tbsp finely grated cheese (optional)
 6 steamed celery strips
 3 cooked carrot pieces
 2 small lettuce leaves

1 Beat egg lightly with water, chopped parsley and other herbs, if using. Mix in the potato and other vegetables, if using.
2 Heat butter in a small frying pan until it foams and pour in the egg mixture. Cook over a medium heat until lightly set, then sprinkle on the cheese, if using.
3 When the omelette is set, slide it out of the frying pan and cut into slices.
4 Reassemble the omelette and decorate.

CHEESY MONSTER *(pages 44 – 45)*

Ingredients for about 8 pieces
 225 g (8 oz) red lentils
 450 ml (¾ pint) water
 1 onion, finely chopped
 15 ml (1 tbsp) oil
 100 g (4 oz) cheese, grated
 1 tsp chopped fresh herbs
 1 egg, beaten
 25 g (1 oz) wholemeal breadcrumbs
  or wheatgerm
 tomato purée and slices of green olive

1 Preheat oven to 190°C (375°F) Gas 5.
2 Cook the lentils in the water until soft and all the liquid has been absorbed.
3 Sauté the onion in the oil until soft.
4 Mix all the ingredients together and press into a greased 23 cm (9 in) sandwich tin.
5 Bake for 30 minutes. Serve hot or cold.

SMILEY FACE PIZZA *(page 46)*

Ingredients for 1 large pizza
 1 onion, chopped
 1 clove garlic, crushed
 15 ml (1 tbsp) oil
 450 g (1 lb) fresh tomatoes, skinned
  and chopped
 30 ml (2 tbsp) tomato purée
 1 tsp chopped fresh oregano or basil
 50 g (2 oz) margarine
 225 g (8 oz) self-raising flour
 50 g (2 oz) cheese, grated
 150 ml (5 fl oz) milk
 small pieces of Mozzarella cheese
 1 slice each of mushroom and green pepper

1 Preheat oven to 200°C (400°F) Gas 6.
2 Sauté the onion and garlic in the oil to soften. Add the tomatoes, purée and herbs Cover and cook gently for 20 minutes.
3 Meanwhile, rub the fat into the flour. Add half the grated cheese and gradually mix in the milk to form a soft dough.
4 Roll out the dough into a 25 cm (10 in) circle. Place on a greased baking tray and sprinkle with the other half of the cheese.
5 Spread the tomato topping mixture over the base and decorate as liked.
6 Bake for about 30 minutes.

QUICHE FLOWER *(page 47)*

Ingredients
 pre-cooked wholemeal pastry case in
  18–20 cm (7–8 in) flan tin
 2 eggs
 300 ml (½ pint) milk
 100 g (4 oz) chopped raw vegetables such
  as leeks, tomatoes and mushrooms
 50 g (2 oz) cheese, grated

1 Preheat oven to 180°C (350°F) Gas 4.
2 Combine the eggs, milk and vegetables.
3 Pour into the flan case, sprinkle with cheese and bake for 20 minutes or until a knife inserted in the centre comes out clean

MEALS WITH FISH

FUNNY FISH

White fish is such a nutritious food that we should all try to eat more on a regular basis and prepared in a variety of ways. Steam it, bake it with herbs and vegetables, poach it in milk or coat it with a cereal mixture for grilling or baking. Double check that there are no bones in the fish before serving. For additional fun, arrange the fish pieces into a shape that your child will recognize. Serve them with crisp and colourful vegetables, such as the swede and fresh cherry tomato used here, and chewy foods like these little dried fruit balls. A slice of wholemeal bread is also a good accompaniment. Make it a rule never to leave your child alone when she is eating since there is always the risk of choking. Besides, meals should be sociable times and not solitary occasions.

Dried fruit balls
These chewy little morsels are made from dried fruit, puffed rice and ground nuts.
(Recipe p. 53)

Funny fish
Brighten up any mealtime with sunny yellow slices of swede filled with poached fish and topped off with a bright red tomato.
(Recipe p. 53)

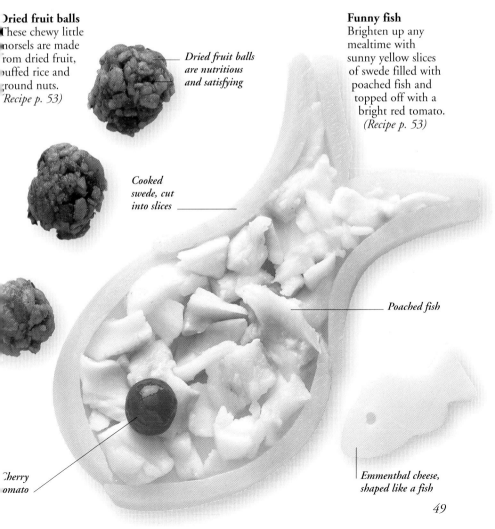

Dried fruit balls are nutritious and satisfying

Cooked swede, cut into slices

Poached fish

Cherry tomato

Emmenthal cheese, shaped like a fish

49

FISH FINGER TREE

White fish is an excellent source of protein, delicate in flavour, low in fat, soft to eat and very easy for young children to digest. Try to buy fresh, not frozen fish and remove the skin and bones before serving (easier done after cooking). The fish finger for this tree is homemade, but good commercial brands are available. Check the list of ingredient on the label and remove the coating if it ha artificial colouring. You can make your ow attractive and nutritious coatings with an combination of grains, cereals, seeds or dr breadcrumbs. Remember to let the grille or baked fish cool down before serving it.

Fish finger tree
Form the trunk of this sturdy tree from a homemade fish finger with a crunchy coating. Arrange bright green steamed broccoli florets around it for the branches and cherry tomatoes as colourful flowers. *(Recipe p. 53)*

Fruity flower
Use a special cutter to shape the melon-ball centre of this flower. Surround it with juicy segments of fresh orange and give it a melon slice for the stem.

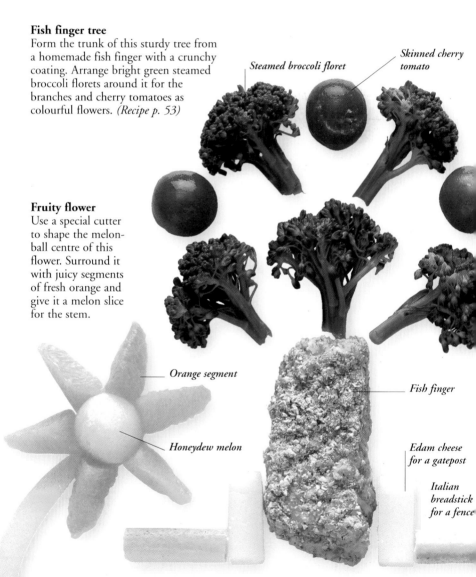

Steamed broccoli floret

Skinned cherry tomato

Orange segment

Fish finger

Honeydew melon

Edam cheese for a gatepost

Italian breadstick for a fence

JUMPING PRAWNS

Prawns are frequently great favourites with children: they're easy to hold, an appealing colour and good to chew on. However, it's best to avoid serving shellfish to children under 12 months old, since it can cause an allergic reaction if eaten too early. Tomatoes (like potatoes) make excellent containers.

Fill them with any ingredients and serve as a lucky dip. Since tomatoes are a rich source of vitamin C and are available fresh all year around, you should try to serve them often in a variety of ways. The fruit pastie dessert is cut open to make a butterfly shape and show off its colourful filling.

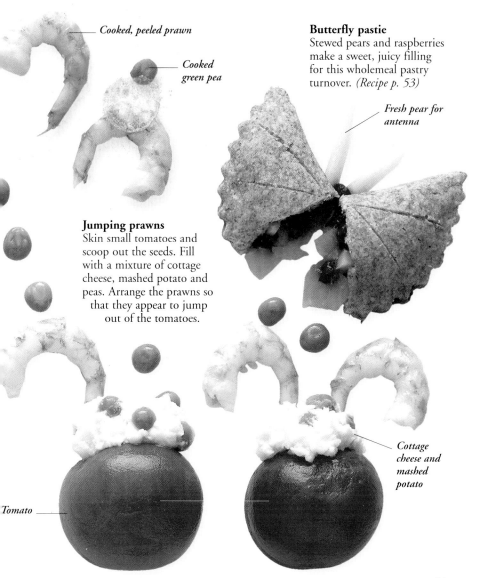

Cooked, peeled prawn

Cooked green pea

Butterfly pastie
Stewed pears and raspberries make a sweet, juicy filling for this wholemeal pastry turnover. *(Recipe p. 53)*

Fresh pear for antenna

Jumping prawns
Skin small tomatoes and scoop out the seeds. Fill with a mixture of cottage cheese, mashed potato and peas. Arrange the prawns so that they appear to jump out of the tomatoes.

Cottage cheese and mashed potato

Tomato

TUNA POTATO BOAT

Scrubbed potatoes, baked in their skins and stuffed with a variety of fillings, served with a few vegetables or a small salad, provide a complete, balanced meal for any member of the family. This boat is filled with scooped-out potato mixed with tuna fish and yoghurt (cottage or curd cheese or Quark would do just as well). Alternatively, make up a filling using a variety of different vegetables, some grated cheese, minced meat or flaked white fish. The potato will have cooled down to the right temperature for your child to eat by the time you have prepared the filling. Dessert is slices of fresh papaya. Try to serve some fresh fruit with every meal so that it becomes a healthy lifetime habit.

Potato boat with three funnels
Give this tuna fish- and yoghurt-stuffed potato boat extra appeal with three jolly funnels made of carrot, swede and celery.

Peeled, seedless grapes for puffs of smoke

Steamed carrot funnel

Baked swede funnel

Flaked tuna with yoghurt and potato

Steamed celery funnel

Baked potato

Peeled papaya slice

FISH RECIPES

FUNNY FISH *(page 49)*

Ingredients for 1 serving
small knob of butter
1 undyed smoked haddock, about
175 g (6 oz)
45 ml (3 tbsp) milk
45 ml (3 tbsp) water
1 fresh or dried bay leaf
slices of peeled, cooked swede
1 cherry tomato

1 Lightly butter the inside of a saucepan.
2 Place the haddock in the pan. Add the milk and water to just cover the fish and the bay leaf. Bring slowly to the boil.
3 Simmer very gently for 5–10 minutes until the fish flakes easily with a knife.
4 Take the fish out of the pan, using a slotted spoon, remove any skin and bones and flake into bite-sized pieces.
5 Decorate with the swede and tomato.

DRIED FRUIT BALLS *(page 49)*

Ingredients for about 20 balls
50 g (2 oz) margarine
175 g (6 oz) dried fruit such as sultanas
or chopped apricots, prunes or dates
2 eggs, beaten
75 g (3 oz) puffed rice cereal
65 g (2½ oz) ground nuts

1 Melt the margarine in a large saucepan over a gentle heat.
2 Stir in the dried fruit and beaten eggs, mix well and heat until thickened (about 10 minutes), but do not allow the mixture to boil or the eggs will scramble.
3 Stir in the cereal and nuts. Leave to cool and then shape into about 20 small balls.
4 Place the fruit balls on a baking sheet, cover and chill until firm.
5 Store between sheets of greaseproof paper in an airtight container in the refrigerator.
6 Note: not suitable for children under 12 months or who are allergic to eggs.

FISH FINGER TREE *(page 50)*

Ingredients for about 16 fish fingers
450 g (1 lb) white fish fillets
75 g (3 oz) yellow cornmeal or wheatgerm
35 g (1½ oz) sesame seeds
1 tsp paprika
2 eggs, beaten
30 ml (2 tbsp) sunflower oil
steamed broccoli and cherry tomatoes

1 Preheat oven to 180°C (350°F) Gas 4.
2 Cut the fish fillets into 3 x 10 cm (1 x 4 in) fingers.
3 Combine the cereal, seeds and paprika.
4 Whisk the eggs and oil together.
5 Roll each fish finger in the cereal mixture, then soak in the egg mixture. Roll again in the cereal until well coated.
6 Place on a greased baking sheet and bake in the oven for 10 minutes, turning the fish after 5 minutes to cook evenly.
7 Decorate with broccoli and tomatoes.

BUTTERFLY PASTIE *(page 51)*

Ingredients for 2 pasties
75 g (3 oz) margarine or butter
175 g (6 oz) wholemeal flour
20 ml (1½ tbsp) water
50 g (2 oz) stewed pears, diced
25 g (1 oz) fresh raspberries
a little beaten egg

1 Preheat oven to 200°C (400°F) Gas 6.
2 Rub the fat into the flour until the mixture resembles fine breadcrumbs.
3 Add the water a little at a time so the mixture binds together but is not sticky.
4 Roll out the pastry on a floured board to a thickness of about 3 mm (⅛ in). Cut into oval shapes with a pastry cutter.
5 Mix the pear and raspberries and divide between the shapes. Brush the edges with beaten egg, fold over and seal.
6 Place the pasties on a greased baking sheet and bake for 15–20 minutes.

MEALS WITH MEAT

PASTIE CRAB

Although it is best to use wholemeal pastry most of the time, puff pastry can make a light and airy change. This plump pastie is filled with an appetizing mixture of cooked chicken, spinach and tiny cauliflower florets but any combination of vegetables, meat, fish or cheeses will do. Test that the centre is completely cooled before serving the pastie to your child, cut crossways into pieces to make it finger food. Pastry is an excellent standby for savoury or dessert dishes and is a useful item to have in the freezer. Prepare it in small batches to freeze or alternatively buy an additive-free commercial brand. Use the pastry to make tart cases, filled pies and pasties and any variety of shaped bases.

Wholemeal pastry

Pastie crab with meat and vegetables
Thinly roll out ready-made puff pastry, fill with any cooked meat and vegetables and bake in a hot oven until golden. Turn the pastie into a crab with claws of wholemeal pastry and Edam cheese.

Orange starfish
Remove all the pith and pips from fresh orange segments and arrange them to look like a starfish.

Chicken, spinach and cauliflower filling

Edam cheese for claws

Soft cheese shell
Shape a spoonful of ricotta cheese into a shell by using a tiny mould lined with clingfilm. This makes it easier to turn out the cheese.

CHICKEN CHEWS

The first meat a child tries is often chicken and it frequently remains a firm favourite. Served as it is here, it becomes a meal that the whole family will enjoy. Simply cut your child's portion into bite-sized, easy-to-handle pieces and arrange them in a funny shape. Choose skinned and boned chicken breast. It is always important to remove the skin since it can be hard to chew and most of the fat lies immediately beneath it. Coat the meat in beaten egg and a ground cereal mixture, breadcrumbs or cornmeal before baking and serve a green vegetable with it. Assorted chopped fresh fruit, served in half an orange with the flesh scooped out, makes a tempting and colourful dessert.

Chicken chews
Arrange crunchily coated chicken pieces with green beans and sautéed potatoes to make this amusing caterpillar. *(Recipe p. 62)*

Orange basket of fresh fruits
Fill an orange shell with peeled and seedless orange segments, strawberries and peeled, seedless green grapes.

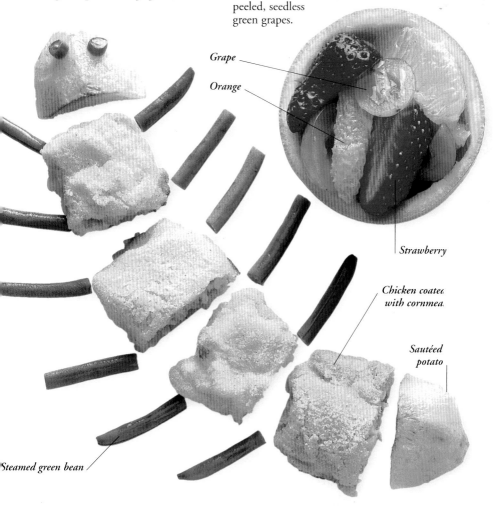

Grape

Orange

Strawberry

Chicken coated with cornmeal

Sautéed potato

Steamed green bean

TASTY TEDDY BEAR

The teddy bear is a favourite shape with all children and one they will recognize from an early age. This is an ideal meal to prepare whenever you've cooked turkey or chicken for your family and pieces are left over, but don't be tempted to use cooked meat that is more than 24 hours old: it may harbour harmful bacteria that will make your child ill. The teddy bear is made from a chopped turkey and mashed potato mixture that is coated with oatmeal and baked in the oven. You can easily adapt the recipe to use any ingredients you have to hand such as flaked fish, mashed cooked pulses or minced lean meat. Serve with a steamed fresh vegetable and slices of juicy fresh fruit.

Tasty teddy bear
A favourite toy becomes an edible mealtime treat when made with turkey or chicken croquettes for its head and body and steamed carrots for its ears, eyes, nose, limbs and colourful buttons. *(Recipe p. 62)*

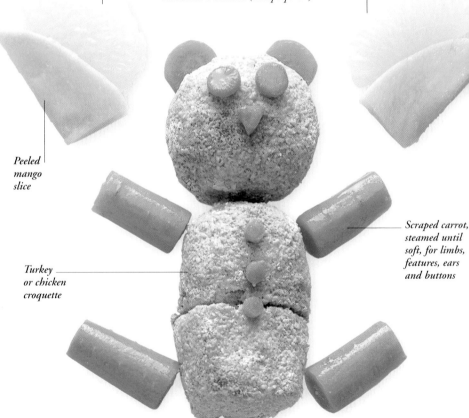

Citrus fruits are rich in vitamin C

Grapefruit segment without pith and seeds

Peeled mango slice

Scraped carrot, steamed until soft, for limbs, features, ears and buttons

Turkey or chicken croquette

MERRY MEATBALL PONY

Small meatballs are a perfect finger food and simple to prepare, particularly if you are making them for the rest of the family. Use best-quality minced lean beef or lamb: it is worth the cost for the flavour and lack of fat. You can bind the meatballs with egg and other ingredients such as rolled oats, wheatgerm or wholemeal breadcrumbs and flavour them with grated cheese or herbs of your choice. Grill or bake the meatballs to give them a crunchy coating and steam or stir-fry the accompanying vegetables so that they retain valuable nutrients as well as their crispness and colour. To add interest in the dessert, top a slightly sweetened oat biscuit with fruit and ricotta or natural yoghurt.

Merry meatball pony
Arrange three crunchily coated mini meatballs with steamed or stir-fried carrots to produce this friendly creature. Mustard and cress "grass" on the side adds extra interest. *(Recipe p. 62)*

Oat biscuit dessert
A homemade biscuit becomes a wholesome dessert when topped with slices of peeled ripe plum and ricotta or natural yoghurt. *(Recipe p. 62)*

Oat biscuit

Steamed carrot triangles for ears

Natural yoghurt

Meatballs for the body and head

Peeled ripe yellow plum

Steamed carrot strips for legs

Mustard and cress for grass

MEAT LOAF MOTOR CAR

A slice of meat loaf forms almost a meal in itself with its blend of meat, vegetables and cereal. Whenever you make a meat loaf for the family, you can cut off a piece for your child and shape it quickly and easily, or use biscuit cutters for fancy shapes. Add a few vegetables for extra colour and flavour. You can even arrange them in the loaf to make patterns by packing the meat mixture into the tin with alternating layers of chopped vegetables such as carrot rings, green peas or sliced mushrooms. If you don't have any meat loaf, simply make this car shape from a slice of bread spread with cooked chicken livers mashed with some natural yoghurt and decorated with strips of cucumber or green beans. For a treat, bake a wholemeal sponge cake with a layer of sliced fruit on the bottom for extra moisture and interest. Cut it into small pieces for serving.

Meat loaf motor car
Form a sturdy motor car from slices of meat loaf, then give it wheels of steamed green courgette. Arrange juicy chicory leaves to make the road.
(Recipe p. 62)

Wholemeal sponge
Arrange small pieces of wholemeal sponge cake beneath the car to represent a bridge. Bite-sized chunks of fruit in the cake are a succulent surprise.
(Recipe p. 63)

Meat loaf

Steamed courgette

Chicory leaf

Pineapple

Glacé cherry

Cake

RATTLE MUNCH

This extra-nutritious beefburger is a tasty mixture of lean minced meat, bulgar wheat, grated cheese or shredded vegetables such as courgettes for moisture and mixed herbs for flavour. Give the beefburger added texture and fibre with a coating of cooked brown rice (as here), barley, rolled oats, wheatgerm or sesame seeds before baking or grilling it.

Copying the shape of your child's favourite rattle or toy will make the meal even more tempting. Since most children enjoy meat presented like this, serve it with vegetables that are colourful and full of flavour so that they don't get overlooked. A yoghurt and fruit purée mousse provides a softer texture after the more chewy savoury course.

Fruit mousse
For an attractive presentation, set single servings of yoghurt and raspberry purée mousse in tiny moulds. *(Recipe p. 63)*

Rattle munch
Recreate a favourite toy with a cereal-coated beefburger, cherry tomatoes, unstuffed stoned green olives and sweet potato. *(Recipe p. 63)*

Unstuffed stoned green olive

Beefburger

Boiled and peeled sweet potato

Skinned cherry tomato

Grape juice drink
Dilute unsweetened red grape juice with water to make a richly coloured and flavourful drink.

LIVER LOG CABIN

Since liver is such a rich source of iron, do try to prepare it for your child regularly. For tenderness and flavour, use calf's or lamb's liver: about 50 g (2 oz), thinly sliced, should be enough. Take care to avoid overcooking the liver or it will become dry, leathery and unappetizing. Gently grill or flash-fry it so it is brown on the outside and only very slightly pink inside. Serve with a sauce such as fresh tomato to add moistness. For speed simply sieve a halved tomato over the liver. This will remove the skin and pips and help to cool the liver down. The sieved tomato and dessert kiwi fruit are both good sources of vitamin C. Try to serve iron-rich foods, particularly grains and pulses, with those that are rich in vitamin C because this helps the body to absorb iron more efficiently.

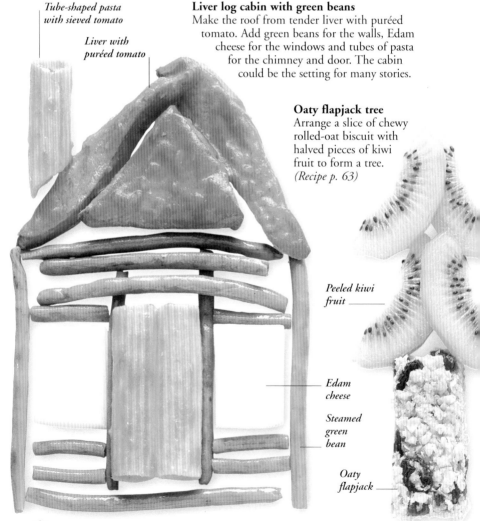

Tube-shaped pasta with sieved tomato

Liver with puréed tomato

Liver log cabin with green beans
Make the roof from tender liver with puréed tomato. Add green beans for the walls, Edam cheese for the windows and tubes of pasta for the chimney and door. The cabin could be the setting for many stories.

Oaty flapjack tree
Arrange a slice of chewy rolled-oat biscuit with halved pieces of kiwi fruit to form a tree.
(Recipe p. 63)

Peeled kiwi fruit

Edam cheese

Steamed green bean

Oaty flapjack

PICK-UP PASTA BOAT

Pasta is an excellent finger food. It is so easy to pick up and available in a wide variety of attractive shapes and colours: the shells that are used for this boat get their green colour from spinach, but you could choose a pale orange variety (made with tomato) or wholemeal pasta instead. Serve it hot or cold with any kind of sauce. This simple bolognese mixture is prepared from lean minced beef,

tomatoes and finely chopped onion, celery and carrot. If you wish, add fresh or dried herbs for even more flavour. Equally good sauces can be made from red, green or brown lentils, minced skinless chicken or turkey, cheese and virtually any chopped or puréed vegetable. Triangles of cheese for sails and chunks of juicy fresh pineapple arranged as a sun complete this nautical scene.

Pick-up pasta boat
Tempt your child to this traditional meal of pasta with bolognese sauce by arranging it as a picture-book sailboat. The pasta and triangles of Gouda cheese can be eaten as a finger food or used to scoop up the bolognese sauce. *(Recipe p. 63)*

Green pepper flag

Pineapple sun
Make a brightly shining sun with chunks of peeled ripe pineapple.

Sliced Gouda sail

Spinach pasta shell

Bolognese sauce

MEAT RECIPES

CHICKEN CHEWS *(page 55)*

Ingredients for about 16 chews
450 g (1 lb) boned raw chicken breast
75 g (3 oz) cornmeal (or other cereal)
35 g (1½ oz) sesame seeds
1 tsp paprika
2 eggs, beaten
30 ml (2 tbsp) sunflower oil

1 Preheat oven to 180°C (350°F) Gas 4.
2 Cut the chicken into bite-sized cubes.
3 Coat and bake as described in the recipe for Fish Finger Tree *(see p. 53)*.

TEDDY CROQUETTE *(page 56)*

Ingredients for about 8 pieces
25 g (1 oz) onion, chopped
25 g (1 oz) celery, chopped
3 tbsp chopped parsley
100 g (4 oz) cooked potato, mashed with
  150 ml (5 fl oz) milk
350 g (12 oz) minced cooked turkey
  (or chicken)
25 g (1 oz) flour
1 egg, beaten with 15 ml (1 tbsp) milk
75 g (3 oz) oatmeal (or other cereal)

1 Preheat oven to 180°C (350°F) Gas 4.
2 Mix together the first 5 ingredients and chill until ready to use.
3 Divide into 8 and shape as desired.
4 Dip each portion into the flour and then the egg before coating in the cereal.
5 Bake for about 10 minutes, turning over after 5 minutes to ensure even browning.

MERRY MEATBALL PONY *(page 57)*

Ingredients for 20–30 meatballs
450 g (1 lb) lean minced beef
50 g (2 oz) rolled oats
1 small onion, finely chopped
1 egg, beaten
50 g (2 oz) grated cheese
1 tsp chopped parsley or oregano

1 Preheat oven to 180°C (350°F) Gas 4.
2 Mix all the ingredients together.
3 With wet hands, shape the mixture into balls about 2.5 cm (1 in) in diameter.
4 Place on a lightly greased baking tray and cook, uncovered, until lightly browned, about 20 minutes. Turn after 10 minutes to ensure even browning.

OAT BISCUIT DESSERT *(page 57)*

Ingredients for 15–20 biscuits
175 g (6 oz) flour
35 g (1½ oz) coarse oatmeal
1 tsp baking powder
75 g (3 oz) butter or margarine
50 g (2 oz) sugar
45 ml (3 tbsp) milk

1 Preheat oven to 180°C (350°F) Gas 4.
2 Mix the first 3 ingredients together.
3 Rub in the fat until the mixture resembles fine breadcrumbs.
4 Stir in the sugar and add the milk.
5 Roll out thinly and cut into shapes.
6 Place on a lightly greased baking tray and bake for 20 minutes.

MEAT LOAF CAR *(page 58)*

Ingredients for 1 small meat loaf
225 g (8 oz) lean minced beef
1 onion, finely chopped
2 celery stalks, chopped
2 carrots, grated
1 clove garlic, crushed
1 egg, beaten
1 tsp ground cumin
2 tbsp chopped fresh parsley
1 tbsp grated Parmesan cheese
1 tbsp wholemeal breadcrumbs or
  wheatgerm

1 Preheat oven to 180°C (350°F) Gas 4.
2 Mix all the ingredients thoroughly together, then pack into a small loaf tin.
3 Bake for about 1 hour.

WHOLEMEAL SPONGE *(page 58)*

Ingredients for 2 layers
100 g (4 oz) soft margarine
100 g (4 oz) sugar
2 eggs, beaten
100 g (4 oz) wholemeal self-raising flour
50 g (2 oz) glacé cherries, halved
50 g (2 oz) pineapple chunks

1 Preheat oven to 180°C (350°F) Gas 4.
2 Line two 18 cm (7 in) sandwich tins with greased paper.
3 Cream the fat and sugar together until smooth and light.
4 Gradually mix in the eggs and flour, keeping the mixture smooth.
5 Divide the fruit between the tins. Spoon half the mixture into each tin and spread level. Bake for 15–20 minutes until firm. Turn out onto a wire tray. Leave to cool.

RATTLE MUNCH *(page 59)*

Ingredients for about 8 pieces
450 g (1 lb) lean minced beef
50 g (2 oz) bulgar wheat
1 small onion, finely chopped
1 egg, beaten
50 g (2 oz) grated cheese (or shredded moist vegetable such as courgette)
1 tsp chopped mixed herbs
100 g (4 oz) cooked brown rice (or other cooked grain)

1 Preheat oven to 180°C (350°F) Gas 4.
2 Mix all the ingredients except the rice.
3 Shape into flat rounds.
4 Roll each round in the cooked rice.
5 Place on a lightly greased baking tray, cover with foil and bake for 20 minutes. Remove the foil for the last 5 minutes.

FRUIT MOUSSE *(page 59)*

Ingredients
1 envelope unflavoured gelatine or vegetarian substitute such as agar-agar
50 ml (2 fl oz) cold water
100 ml (4 fl oz) boiling water

225 ml (8 fl oz) unsweetened fruit juice
225 g (8 oz) puréed fruit
150 ml (5 fl oz) natural yoghurt

1 Pour cold water into a bowl. Sprinkle on the gelatine. Leave to soak for 1 minute.
2 Add the boiling water to the bowl and stir to dissolve the gelatine.
3 Mix in the fruit juice, fruit and yoghurt.
4 Pour into moulds and chill until firm.

OATY FLAPJACK TREE *(page 60)*

Ingredients for 15–20 pieces
225 g (8 oz) rolled oats or muesli
75 g (3 oz) sugar
1 tsp baking powder
150 g (5 oz) butter, melted
100 g (4 oz) dried fruit and orange peel

1 Preheat oven to 150°C (300°F) Gas 2.
2 Mix the cereal, sugar and baking powder together.
3 Add the melted butter and dried fruit and peel, and mix well together.
4 Pat the mixture into an ungreased 20 x 30 cm (8 x 12 in) baking tray. Bake for about 20 minutes until golden brown. Cut into squares and allow to cool.

PICK-UP PASTA BOAT *(page 61)*

Ingredients for bolognese sauce
1 tsp oil
1 small onion, finely chopped
1 celery stalk, finely chopped
1 small carrot, finely chopped
450 g (1 lb) lean minced beef
15 ml (1 tbsp) tomato purée
150 ml (¼ pint) beef or vegetable stock
420 g (15 oz) can chopped tomatoes

1 Heat the oil and fry the onion, celery and carrot until softened and golden.
2 Add the minced beef and cook until browned. Add the tomato purée and cook for 1 minute.
3 Pour in the stock and tomatoes, mix well and bring to the boil.
4 Simmer over a low heat for 45 minutes.

VEGETABLE MEALS

TRAFFIC LIGHTS

The preparation for this meal need not be time consuming if you have some vegetable purées in the freezer and a good assortment of pasta shapes. You can arrange purées and thick sauces in perfect circles by shaping them in a plain round pastry cutter. The jelly car is made from a simple recipe and shaped with a small biscuit cutter. This kind of meal will appeal to your child by making food interesting and enjoyable to eat.

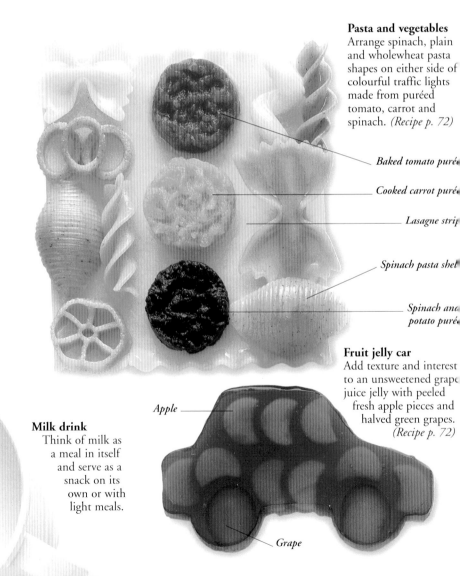

Pasta and vegetables
Arrange spinach, plain and wholewheat pasta shapes on either side of colourful traffic lights made from puréed tomato, carrot and spinach. *(Recipe p. 72)*

Baked tomato purée

Cooked carrot purée

Lasagne strip

Spinach pasta shell

Spinach and potato purée

Fruit jelly car
Add texture and interest to an unsweetened grape juice jelly with peeled fresh apple pieces and halved green grapes. *(Recipe p. 72)*

Apple

Milk drink
Think of milk as a meal in itself and serve as a snack on its own or with light meals.

Grape

BIRD'S NEST FEAST

A colourful arrangement and a variety of textures make this meal attractive, and it has lots of things to pick up and eat as finger foods. The fruity bird is sitting on a nest that contains falafel, a tasty Middle-Eastern dish made from cooked chick peas mashed, flavoured, mixed with soft breadcrumbs or other cereal and rolled into balls. For extra crunch, they can be coated with wheatgerm before baking. They are delicious served with a sauce of yoghurt and chopped fresh mint, or yoghurt and tahini (sesame paste). The salad nest is made from thin strips of wholemeal pitta bread, raw red cabbage and lettuce, but any bread strips and shredded raw or cooked vegetables would do.

Fruity bird with fantail
Soaked sultanas decorate a halved peach for the bird's head and body, while chunks of fresh pineapple give it a perky fantail.

Falafel ball eggs in a leafy nest
Sit the bird in a nest of lettuce, red cabbage and pitta bread, on bite-sized eggs formed from chick-pea falafel balls. *(Recipe p. 72)*

Fresh pineapple

Soaked sultanas

Fresh peach, peeled and stoned

Shredded lettuce

Falafel balls

Pitta bread strips

Shredded red cabbage

BEANY RING

Cooked beans mix well with all kinds of meat or vegetable stews, bakes and casseroles. For speed, you can use drained, canned beans or beans in tomato sauce (check the label for added sugar and salt). Heat up with small pieces of assorted cooked vegetables and serve in a ring of mashed potato, pasta or cooked grains. Here, cooked brown rice was mixed with aduki beans and pressed into a ring mould. Shape with a cup or a shallow glass if you don't have a mould.

Beany ring with mixed vegetables
This wholesome flower has a centre of red kidney beans, celery and cauliflower florets cooked in a tomato sauce, ringed by aduki beans with brown rice and celery.

Red kidney bean

Celery

Tomato sauce

Cauliflower floret

Steamed celery

Brown rice mixed with aduki beans

Strawberry milkshake
Milk blended with crushed strawberries is always a favourite summer drink.

Cooking dried pulses
These edible seeds of pod vegetables are cheap, rich in protein, iron and minerals and low in fats. Most need presoaking for 8–12 hours (lentils are the exception).

Red kidney beans need fast boiling for at least 10 minutes to destroy their toxins.

Black-eyed beans absorb flavours well.

Chick peas must be cooked until soft.

Pinto beans turn pale pink when cooked.

Flageolet beans taste good and look pretty.

Cannellini beans are delicious served in tomato sauce.

Soya beans must be boiled fast for the first hour of cooking.

Aduki beans are good mixed with rice.

Split peas are perfect for soups and purées.

Haricot beans are the original baked beans.

Lentils (either whole or split) do not need soaking and are easy for children to digest.

Butter beans have a mild taste. They keep their shape well and are ideal to serve as a finger food.

POLKA-DOT OCTOPUS

This salad is a fun and appealing way to serve beans, but do take care when first introducing them to your child. Cook the beans very thoroughly and serve in small portions until your child's sensitive digestive system is accustomed to them. Once you are familiar with the many kinds, try to use beans frequently in salads, soups, casseroles, fillings and purées. They are colourful, rich in protein and pick up the flavours of other foods well. This bean salad includes diced raw vegetables that you can vary according to what you have available, and is served in a bread roll. When possible, cook different kinds of bean together to get a variety of flavours, textures and colours in one dish.

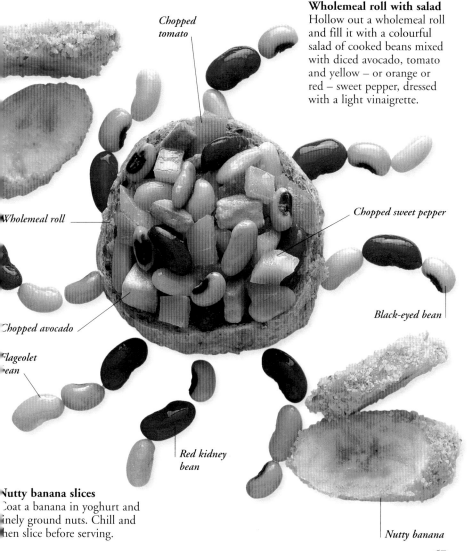

Chopped tomato

Wholemeal roll with salad
Hollow out a wholemeal roll and fill it with a colourful salad of cooked beans mixed with diced avocado, tomato and yellow – or orange or red – sweet pepper, dressed with a light vinaigrette.

Wholemeal roll

Chopped sweet pepper

Chopped avocado

Black-eyed bean

Flageolet bean

Red kidney bean

Nutty banana slices
Coat a banana in yoghurt and finely ground nuts. Chill and then slice before serving.

Nutty banana

LEAFY PARCEL TRAIN

You can certainly involve older children in preparing these vegetable parcels. Younger ones will be intrigued simply by the idea of wrapping something up and unwrapping it again. Here, cabbage leaves are used as the wrapping: an outer leaf, an inner leaf and a leaf of red cabbage. Spinach leaves would do just as well. You can fill them with any finely diced vegetables mixed with cooked grains and cheese (mushrooms, leeks, celery, pot barley and soft cheese are used here). The parcels are then oven baked in stock reserved from cooking the grains. Fresh apple rings, celery and steamed carrots add crunchy texture and complete the picture of an old-fashioned steam locomotive.

Apple-ring steam clouds
Use fancy biscuit cutters to shape peeled and cored fresh apple rings into clouds of steam.

Leafy parcel train
For even more realism, give the train's engine a funnel of raw celery, and position five carrot slices as wheels under the engine and rolling stock of leafy parcels. *(Recipe p. 72)*

Outer cabbage leaf

Inner cabbage leaf

Raw celery

Red cabbage leaf

Steamed carrot slice

VEGETABLE ROCKET

Courgettes, tomatoes and peppers are ideal for stuffing. Although a vegetarian mixture is used here, you could include any leftover minced lean meat or skinless chicken in the basic rice filling. If you are not preparing this dish for the rest of the family, you can speed up the cooking process by slicing the courgette in half lengthwise, steaming it and then mixing the pulp with the chosen filling, adding a little tahini (sesame paste) or yoghurt to bind the mixture. The meal is made more substantial with a small slice of wholemeal bread spread with low-fat cheese, a pear slice cut to resemble a moon and a tart for dessert containing slices of fresh and dried fruits to dip into its yoghurt filling.

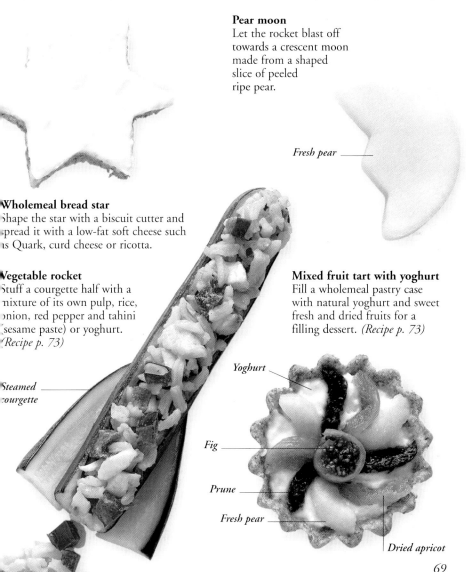

Pear moon
Let the rocket blast off
towards a crescent moon
made from a shaped
slice of peeled
ripe pear.

Fresh pear _____

Wholemeal bread star
Shape the star with a biscuit cutter and spread it with a low-fat soft cheese such as Quark, curd cheese or ricotta.

Vegetable rocket
Stuff a courgette half with a mixture of its own pulp, rice, onion, red pepper and tahini (sesame paste) or yoghurt. *(Recipe p. 73)*

Steamed _____
courgette

Mixed fruit tart with yoghurt
Fill a wholemeal pastry case with natural yoghurt and sweet fresh and dried fruits for a filling dessert. *(Recipe p. 73)*

Yoghurt _____

Fig _____

Prune _____

Fresh pear _____

Dried apricot

STIR-FRIED KITE

Stir-frying is the healthy Chinese method of cooking foods very quickly in very little oil so that they retain all their goodness. A wok is the traditional vessel for stir-frying but you can use a small frying pan over a high heat. Use just a little polyunsaturated vegetable oil and whatever fresh vegetables you have available; any combination will make a tasty dish for your child. Cubes of firm tofu (soya bean curd) are added to the stir-fry shown here. It is an ideal food for young children (and for all the family too) since it is soft, mild in flavour, easy to digest and rich in protein and calcium. Wholemeal pitta bread, cut to look like a kite, and fresh banana balance the meal perfectly.

Stir-fried kite with tofu
This colourful all-in-one meal of stir-fried red and yellow sweet peppers, courgette strips, beansprouts and Chinese cabbage is given extra nutritional value with cubes of firm tofu, wholemeal pitta bread and chunks of ripe banana.

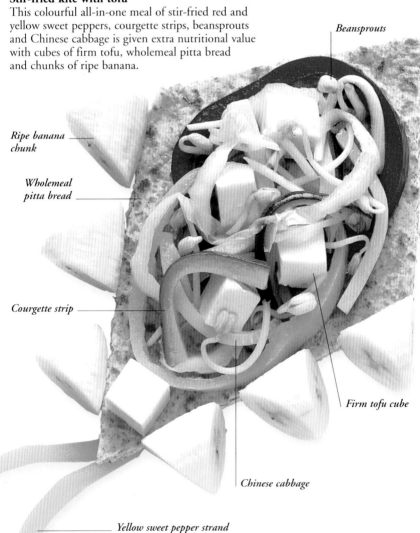

Beansprouts

Ripe banana chunk

Wholemeal pitta bread

Courgette strip

Firm tofu cube

Chinese cabbage

Yellow sweet pepper strand

SAVOURY CONE

A leftover piece of wholemeal pastry dough, shaped and baked quickly in a hot oven, provides the base for this savoury cone. The topping is made from any grated vegetables, but including cooked beetroot to give it a vibrant colour, bound together with a blend of natural yoghurt, mayonnaise and ground almonds. Soft curd cheese or Quark would be speedy alternatives if time is short. The decoratively shaped pieces of fresh fruit and cheese are cut out with miniature biscuit cutters. These finger foods allow children to choose which item to eat first at their own pace and help in the development of hand-to-mouth co-ordination. They can also be used as dippers in the soft topping.

Savoury cone with soft topping
For this fun presentation, set a blend of grated cooked beetroot, ground almonds, yoghurt and mayonnaise – shaped with an ice-cream scoop – atop a piece of wholemeal pastry. *(Recipe p. 73)*

Gouda cheese

Apple

Apple

Mango

Melon

Melon

Mango

Wholemeal pastry

Gouda cheese

Kiwi fruit

VEGETABLE RECIPES

TRAFFIC LIGHTS *(page 64)*

Ingredients
2 medium tomatoes
75 g (3 oz) carrot
100 g (4 oz) spinach, well washed
1 small potato
150 ml (5 fl oz) milk
small knob of butter (optional)

1 Preheat oven to 180°C (350°F) Gas 4.
2 Cut a cross in the tops of the tomatoes. Place on a lightly greased baking sheet and bake for 25 minutes.
3 Steam the carrot and spinach until soft.
4 Boil the potato until soft.
5 Sieve the tomatoes to remove skin and pips, or purée and then sieve.
6 Purée the carrot with the milk. Mix in the butter, if using.
7 Purée the spinach with the potato.

FRUIT JELLY CAR *(page 64)*

Ingredients
50 ml (2 fl oz) cold water
1 envelope unflavoured gelatine or
*   vegetarian substitute such as agar-agar*
100 ml (4 fl oz) boiling water
225 ml (8 fl oz) unsweetened fruit juice
225 g (8 oz) apples, peeled and chopped
*   (or other fresh fruit)*
handful of green grapes, halved

1 Pour cold water into a bowl. Sprinkle on the gelatine. Leave to soak for 1 minute.
2 Add the boiling water to the bowl and stir to dissolve the gelatine.
3 Mix in the fruit juice.
4 Arrange the fruit in moulds or on a tray. Carefully pour over enough jelly to cover the fruit. Chill until set.
5 Pour over the rest of the jelly (slightly warm it to liquefy again, if necessary). Chill until set firm.
6 Shape the fruit jelly with a car-shaped biscuit cutter if not set in moulds.

FALAFEL BALL EGGS *(page 65)*

Ingredients for about 20 pieces
275 g (10 oz) chick peas, presoaked
1 onion, finely chopped
1 clove garlic, crushed
45 ml (3 tbsp) tahini (sesame paste)
1 tsp ground cumin
100 g (4 oz) breadcrumbs (or wheatgerm,
*   cooked bulgar wheat or rolled oats)*
1 egg, beaten

1 Boil the chick peas in fresh water until soft (between 1 and 1½ hours) or cook in a pressure cooker for 30 minutes.
2 Preheat oven to 180°C (350°F) Gas 4.
3 Drain the chick peas and mash with the onion and garlic to form a thick pulp.
4 Add the tahini, cumin, breadcrumbs (or cereal) and beaten egg and mix well.
5 Roll the mixture into small balls. Place on a greased baking tray and bake for 15–20 minutes.

LEAFY PARCEL TRAIN *(page 68)*

Ingredients for 8 parcels
100 g (4 oz) pot barley
2 leeks, chopped
2 celery stalks, chopped
8 cabbage leaves
100 g (4 oz) mushrooms, chopped
50 g (2 oz) soft cheese such as curd or
*   cottage cheese, or grated hard cheese*
1 tsp chopped mixed herbs
1 egg, beaten, to bind if necessary

1 Cover the barley with boiling water and cook for about 40 minutes until soft. Drain, reserving the liquid, and set aside.
2 Preheat oven to 180°C (350°F) Gas 4.
3 Steam the leeks and celery to soften.
4 Cook the cabbage leaves in boiling water for 2 minutes, then drain and pat dry.
5 Mix together the cooked barley, all of the vegetables, the cheese and herbs. If the mixture is too crumbly, bind with the egg.

6 Place about 1 tbsp of the filling on a cabbage leaf, fold the sides into the centre and roll up into a parcel. Repeat with the other cabbage leaves.

7 Place the parcels, seam sides down, in a lightly greased baking dish. Add enough of the reserved barley stock to come half way up the parcels. Cover with foil and bake for about 30 minutes.

VEGETABLE ROCKET *(page 69)*

Ingredients for 8 servings
4 courgettes
1 onion, finely chopped
1 clove garlic, crushed
1 red pepper, deseeded and finely chopped
30 ml (2 tbsp) oil
100 g (4 oz) cooked brown rice (or other grain such as bulgar wheat)
15 ml (1 tbsp) tahini (sesame paste), natural yoghurt or smooth peanut butter
300 ml (½ pint) stock or boiling water

1 Preheat oven to 180°C (350°F) Gas 4.
2 Blanch the courgettes for 3–4 minutes in boiling water.
3 Cut the courgettes in half lengthwise, scoop out the centres (being careful not to pierce the shell) and chop up the pulp.
4 Heat the oil in a small pan. Sauté the onion, garlic, red pepper and courgette pulp for 5 minutes. Mix in the rice (or other grain), then add the tahini, yoghurt or peanut butter to bind the mixture.
5 Arrange the courgette shells in a lightly greased baking dish. Divide the filling evenly between the shells and pour the stock or boiling water around them.
6 Cover with foil and bake for 20 minutes until the vegetables are tender.

MIXED FRUIT TART *(page 69)*

Ingredients for about 8 servings
75 g (3 oz) margarine or butter
175 g (6 oz) wholemeal flour
20 ml (1½ tbsp) water
225 ml (8 fl oz) natural yoghurt
175 g (6 oz) soaked dried fruits such as figs, prunes and apricots, cut in pieces
50 g (2 oz) fresh fruit such as pears, peeled and sliced

1 Preheat oven to 200°C (400°F) Gas 6.
2 Rub the fat into the flour until the mixture resembles fine breadcrumbs.
3 Add the water a little at a time until the mixture binds together. The dough should be soft but not sticky.
4 Roll out the dough on a floured surface until about 3 mm (⅛ in) thick. Cut out circles with a large biscuit cutter (or use a saucer as a guide) and use to line lightly greased individual tart tins.
5 To bake blind, prick the bases with a fork, cover with foil and sprinkle with dried beans. Bake for 15 minutes, then remove the beans and foil and bake for another 5 minutes until brown. Cool.
6 Divide the yoghurt between the cooled pastry cases and arrange the fruits on top.

SAVOURY CONE *(page 71)*

Ingredients for 1 serving
scraps of leftover wholemeal pastry dough from the recipe above
1 tbsp grated cooked beetroot
1 tbsp cooked puréed vegetables such as carrot, swede or sweet potato
1 tbsp ground almonds
2 tsp natural yoghurt
1 tsp mayonnaise

1 Preheat oven to 200°C (400°F) Gas 6.
2 Roll out the pastry, cut to shape and place on a greased baking tray. Bake for 15 minutes until lightly browned. Cool.
3 Mix all the topping ingredients. Arrange with the pastry to form an ice-cream cone.

NUTRITIOUS SOUPS

FRESH PEA SOUP
(recipe p. 75)

BORSCHT
(recipe p. 75)

SPINACH SOUP
(recipe p. 75)

Thick and hearty soups are one of the best meals you can give to your child. They are also very quick and easy to prepare. For a soup made in five minutes, purée any vegetables in a blender and then thin the mixture with water, milk or yoghurt. Serve hot or cold with homemade rusks (see p. 76) if desired. For a thick soup, make a base of cooked pulses or potatoes and add vegetables and liquid. Keep a supply of homemade stock in the freezer and use with any vegetables you have on hand. Small children tend to like their soups rather thick for easier eating.

LENTIL SOUP
(recipe p. 76)

BUTTER BEAN SOUP
(recipe p. 75)

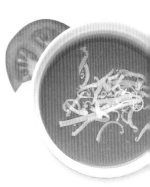

CARROT SOUP
(recipe p. 76)

CHICKEN STOCK SOUP
(recipe p. 76)

FRESH TOMATO SOU
(recipe p. 75)

SOUP RECIPES

FRESH PEA SOUP *(page 74)*

Makes about 1½ litres (2½ pints)
450g (1lb) shelled fresh peas
1 onion, chopped
1 small lettuce, roughly chopped
1 litre (1¾ pints) water or stock
150 ml (5 fl oz) natural yoghurt

1 Simmer the shelled peas, onion and lettuce in the water or stock until the peas are soft, about 20–30 minutes.
2 Liquidize the mixture until smooth.
3 Add the yoghurt to a little of the soup, then combine this mixture with the rest of the soup. Reheat gently, but do not allow to boil or the soup may curdle.

BORSCHT *(page 74)*

Makes about 900 ml (1½ pints)
4 medium cooked beetroots, peeled
600 ml (1 pint) milk
15 ml (1 tbsp) lemon juice
30 ml (2 tbsp) natural yoghurt

1 Purée the cooked beetroot and combine with the milk.
2 Bring the mixture gently to the boil.
3 Remove from the heat and stir in the lemon juice. Serve the soup warm or cold, decorated with a swirl of yoghurt.

SPINACH SOUP *(page 74)*

Makes about 900 ml (1½ pints)
450 g (1 lb) spinach, fresh or frozen
1 small onion, chopped
15 ml (1 tbsp) oil
900 ml (1½ pints) chicken or vegetable stock

1 Wash the spinach thoroughly, or thaw and drain well if frozen.
2 Sauté the onion in the oil to soften.
3 Add the spinach and the stock. Bring to the boil and simmer until tender.
4 Liquidize the mixture until smooth.

BUTTER BEAN SOUP *(page 74)*

Makes about 1 litre (1¾ pints)
15 ml (1 tbsp) oil
1 onion, chopped
1 carrot, chopped
1 celery stalk, chopped
100 g (4 oz) dried butter beans, presoaked
900 ml (1½ pints) stock or water
15 ml (1 tbsp) tomato juice or purée
1 bay leaf

1 Heat the oil and sauté the onion for about 3 minutes to soften.
2 Add the carrot and celery and cook gently for a further 3–4 minutes.
3 Add the drained butter beans, stock or water, tomato juice or purée and the bay leaf. Cover and simmer for 1 hour or cook in a pressure cooker for 20 minutes.
4 Remove the bay leaf and liquidize the mixture until smooth.

FRESH TOMATO SOUP *(page 74)*

Makes about 1 litre (1¾ pints)
25 g (1 oz) margarine
1 onion, sliced
1 clove garlic, crushed
450 g (1 lb) fresh tomatoes, roughly chopped
600 ml (1 pint) stock
150 ml (5 fl oz) milk

1 Melt the margarine and sauté the onion and garlic until soft.
2 Add the tomatoes and stock. Cover and simmer for 15 minutes.
3 Remove from the heat and add the milk.
4 Liquidize the mixture until smooth, then sieve to remove the tomato skins and pips if necessary. Reheat, but do not allow to boil or the soup may curdle.

Soup recipes continued page 76

CHICKEN STOCK SOUP *(page 74)*

Makes about 2 litres (3½ pints)
1 chicken carcass or bones from a cooked
bird (and giblets, if available)
1 onion, sliced
1 carrot, sliced
1 celery stalk, sliced
1 tsp chopped mixed herbs
1 bay leaf
2 litres (3½ pints) water

1 Place the chicken carcass or bones (and giblets), onion, carrot, celery and herbs in a large saucepan. Add the water and bring to the boil. Skim well, cover and then simmer for at least 1 hour.
2 Allow the mixture to cool and then strain, discarding the solids.
3 Use as a stock or reheat and serve as it is with small cubes of bread floating on top.
4 For variety and extra flavour, reheat the stock with peas or diced vegetables.
5 To make the soup more substantial, add some cooked rice, pot barley, noodles or tiny soup pasta shapes.

CARROT SOUP *(page 74)*

Makes about 1 litre (1¾ pints)
450 g (1 lb) carrots, well scrubbed and
roughly chopped
2 celery stalks, chopped
600 ml (1 pint) stock or water
300 ml (½ pint) milk

1 Simmer the carrots and celery in the stock or water for about 15 minutes, until the vegetables are soft.
2 Liquidize the mixture until smooth.
3 Add the milk and reheat gently, but do not allow to boil or the soup may curdle.

LENTIL SOUP *(page 74)*

Makes about 1½ litres (2½ pints)
15 ml (1 tbsp) oil
1 onion, chopped
2 leeks, chopped
2 carrots, sliced
3 celery stalks, chopped
50 g (2 oz) red or brown lentils (or yellow
split peas or pot barley)
15 ml (1 tbsp) tamari (salt-free soya sauce)
1 tsp cumin seeds
1 litre (1 ¾) pints stock or water

1 Heat the oil and sauté the onion, leeks, carrots and celery for about 5 minutes until slightly softened but not browned.
2 Add the lentils (or other pulses), tamari, cumin seeds and water or stock. Bring to the boil, then cover and simmer for about 1 hour or until the lentils and vegetables are very soft.
3 Liquidize until completely smooth.

HOMEMADE RUSKS *(page 74)*

Ingredients
Thick slices of wholewheat or white bread
(bread that is a few days old is fine)

1 Preheat oven to its lowest setting.
2 Cut the bread into fingers, squares or triangles. Alternatively, use biscuit cutters to cut it into attractive shapes.
3 Place the shapes on an ungreased baking tray and bake in the oven for about 1 hour until they are dry, hard and golden brown. Turn them over after 30 minutes so that they colour evenly.
4 Cool thoroughly on a wire rack.
5 Store in an airtight container. They will keep for several days.

SNACKS AND PICNICS

STICKMAN FEAST

Few children will be able to resist this funny figure or its combination of foods. The head is made from a mild version of the Mexican dip, guacamole. Simply add a few drops of chilli sauce, sliced fresh green chillies or powdered chilli for serving to the rest of the family. The dippers can be any selection of scrubbed, sliced fresh vegetables (steam to soften them when serving to children under 12 months of age, particularly small pieces like the carrot features). Pancakes are always popular and can be made in batches for freezing. They're equally good filled with a fruit purée, as here, or savoury mixtures.

Stickman feast
Arrange bread, vegetables and cheese for the body and limbs. The head is a generous portion of guacamole. *(Recipe p. 83)*

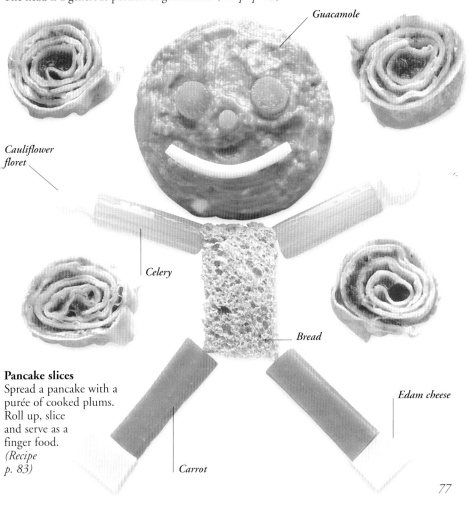

Guacamole

Cauliflower floret

Celery

Bread

Edam cheese

Pancake slices
Spread a pancake with a purée of cooked plums. Roll up, slice and serve as a finger food. *(Recipe p. 83)*

Carrot

SANDWICH MAN

Don't overlook sandwiches as a quick, easy and nutritious meal for your child. Thin slices of wholemeal or other wholegrain bread can be shaped with a decorative metal cutter for fun. Spread with any kind of homemade topping: soft or hard cheeses, grated vegetables and fruits, cooked meats, no-added-sugar jams or bean purées – the choice is endless. Try not to use lots of butter or margarine: a thin scraping is enough (in fact, your child won't even notice if you use none at all on sandwiches). Excess use of butter or margarine is an undesirable habit, learned all too often at a very early age.

Sandwich man

Shape a slice of wholemeal bread with a biscuit cutter, spread with a mixture of curd cheese, chopped dates and watercress and serve on a bed of shredded lettuce.

Fruity building blocks

Make these from chunky cubes of melon: orange Charentais and fragrant yellow cantaloupe.

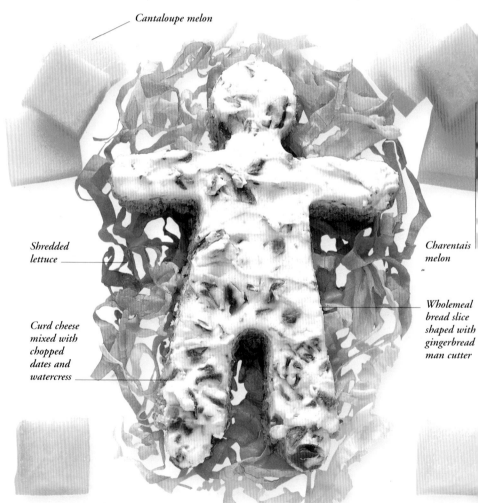

Cantaloupe melon

Shredded lettuce

Charentais melon

Curd cheese mixed with chopped dates and watercress

Wholemeal bread slice shaped with gingerbread man cutter

DIP IDEAS

PEANUT BUTTER OR
TAHINI AND SOFT TOFU

LOW-FAT SOFT CHEESE
AND TOMATO PURÉE

COOKED CHICKEN
LIVERS AND
COTTAGE CHEESE

RIPE AVOCADO AND
COTTAGE CHEESE

Interesting and colourful dips can be
made from a wide variety of savoury
and sweet ingredients, and are a good
way of getting a fussy eater to try new
tastes. Serve dips with raw or lightly
steamed vegetables, homemade rusks
or slices of fruit, but expect young
children to dip their fingers in too.
Use these tasty, nutritious dips as
spreads for sandwiches, toppings for
slices of wholemeal bread or fillings
for tomatoes, celery stalks, sweet
peppers or small pastry cases. Your
child will enjoy the experience of
dipping and tasting and you will find
that the rest of the family are just as
keen to sample these different ideas.

HUMMUS *(recipe p. 83)*

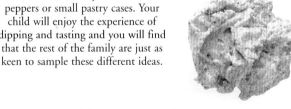

MASHED TUNA FISH
AND CURD CHEESE

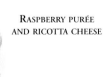

CHOPPED COOKED SPINACH,
CURD CHEESE AND
LEMON JUICE

RASPBERRY PURÉE
AND RICOTTA CHEESE

YOGHURT, GRATED COCONUT AND ORANGE JUICE

BAKING

BANANA OATMEAL CAKE *(recipe p. 83)*

PLAIN OAT BISCUIT *(recipe p. 41)*

WHOLEMEAL SPONGE CAKE *(recipe p. 63)*

There is no good reason why children should have any cakes and biscuits in their first two years of life. However, outside pressure from playgroups and parties will doubtless encourage the inevitable taste for sweet things, so prepare for this by getting your child used to less sugary cakes and biscuits made from unrefined ingredients. For example, substitute the stronger tasting, dark brown, unrefined sugars with molasses to cut down on the amount of sugar required in recipes. Add sweeteners like dried fruits and fruit juices when you can (but avoid honey for children under 12 months old), and try to use wholemeal flour in your baking too.

OATY FLAPJACK *(recipe p. 63)*

WHOLEMEAL FRUIT SCONE WITH YOGHURT AND JAM *(recipe p. 84)*

CARROT CAKE *(recipe p. 84)*

DATE AND NUT CAKE *(recipe p. 84)*

WHOLEMEAL SPONGE WITH CAROB OR COCOA *(recipe p. 84)*

FOOD ON THE MOVE

Most children become restless and bored when strapped into a car seat or taken on a train for any length of time and it's a good idea to take a range of snacks for them to eat so you don't have to keep entertaining them. Don't pack messy foods or things that are difficult to hold. Cut sandwiches, small biscuits and pieces of fruit are best when you are on the move, even if it's just to cheer up your child when you are out shopping with the push-chair. Individual pastry cases are another convenient way to package food when you are travelling with children. Little packets of dried fruit, cubes of hard cheese and raw or lightly steamed vegetable sticks are also good standbys.

Peeled apple slices

Mini sandwiches
Take care not to overfill sandwiches, or they will be messy to eat. Cut into small squares for easy handling.

OATY FLAPJACK SLICE
(recipe p. 63)

MINI QUICHE
FLOWER
(recipe p. 48)

PICNIC FOODS

The best picnics are full of surprises but are simple to unpack and serve. Slice a plain or wholemeal pitta bread and fill the pocket with salad, a homemade spread or thinly sliced lean meat. Cut the bread package into easily handled pieces when you reach your destination. Alternatively, cut a French loaf in half lengthwise, scoop out some of the crumbs and fill with a salad or spread. This can be sliced to make instant sandwiches as soon as you arrive. Assorted dips in tiny pots, plastic bags of prepared vegetables and slices of fresh fruit all provide the variety that makes for the most successful picnics. Don't forget to take along plenty of drink and water as well as a supply of wipes.

Carrot cake
This lightly spiced cake is sweetened with grated carrots. It has a moist texture and won't collapse into crumbs. *(Recipe p. 84)*

Pitta bread sandwich
Pack in the filling so that there's a generous amount and it doesn't fall out. Serve in small pieces that your child can easily hold.

Vegetable sticks
Accompany the cheese and tomato dip with sticks of raw vegetables.

Courgette

Diluted orange drink
Drinks are a must for picnics and travelling. Mix on the spot.

Celery

Sweet pepper

Carrot

Tomato dip
Pack a dip made from curd cheese and tomato into a jar that has a tightly fitting lid.

SNACK AND PICNIC RECIPES

GUACAMOLE *(page 77)*

Ingredients

1 ripe avocado, peeled, stoned and cubed
1 small onion, very finely chopped
1 tomato, peeled and finely chopped
15 ml (1 tbsp) natural yoghurt
juice of 1 lemon

1 Mash the avocado flesh, then combine with the onion, tomato, yoghurt and lemon juice. Mix to blend the ingredients.
2 Cover the dip with clingfilm and chill well before serving.

PANCAKE SLICES *(page 77)*

Ingredients for about 8 pancakes

100 g (4 oz) flour
1 egg
300 ml (½ pint) milk
30 ml (2 tbsp) oil
puréed cooked fruit such as plum

1 Sieve the flour into a bowl.
2 Make a well in the centre and crack the egg into it. Gradually mix in the milk by stirring from the centre and drawing the dry ingredients into the egg and milk.
3 Heat an omelette pan and brush with a few drops of oil.
4 Pour in enough batter to coat the base of the pan. Cook for 1–2 minutes until the underside of the pancake is golden (keep shaking the pan so the pancake remains loose). Turn with a spatula and cook the other side until golden, 1–2 minutes.
5 If cooking for the family, stack the pancakes as you make them, with a sheet of greaseproof paper between each one. Keep warm in a low oven.
6 Spread the pancakes with fruit purée, roll up, and slice before serving.

HUMMUS *(page 79)*

Ingredients

150 g (5 oz) chick peas, presoaked
1 clove garlic, crushed
1 tsp ground cumin
60 ml (4 tbsp) tahini (sesame paste)
60 ml (4 tbsp) lemon juice
15 ml (1 tbsp) water, if necessary

1 Boil the chick peas in fresh water until soft (1–1½ hours) or cook in a pressure cooker for 30 minutes. Drain and cool.
2 Liquidize the cooked chick peas with the garlic, cumin, tahini and lemon juice.
3 Moisten with a little water if needed (it should be the consistency of mayonnaise).

BANANA OATMEAL CAKE *(page 80)*

Ingredients for 1 large cake

75 g (3 oz) rolled oats
225 ml (8 fl oz) milk
275 g (10 oz) flour
50 g (2 oz) sugar
5 tsp baking powder
2 tsp bicarbonate of soda
1 tsp ground cinnamon
1 tsp ground nutmeg
50 ml (2 fl oz) sunflower oil
2 eggs, beaten
2 tsp vanilla extract
4–5 bananas, mashed

1 Preheat oven to 180°C (350°F) Gas 4.
2 Combine the oats and milk. Set aside.
3 Mix the dry ingredients.
4 Add the oil, eggs, vanilla and bananas to the oats and milk. Mix with the dry ingredients until they are just moistened.
5 Fill a greased loaf tin and bake for about 1½ hours. Alternatively, fill small paper cases and bake for about 35 minutes or until golden brown. Cool on a wire rack. This cake is best 2–3 days after making.

Snack and picnic recipes continued page 84

WHOLEMEAL SCONES WITH FRUIT OR CHEESE *(page 80)*

Ingredients for about 10 scones
50 g (2 oz) butter or margarine
225 g (8 oz) wholemeal self-raising flour
50 g (2 oz) dried fruit or grated cheese
150 ml (5 fl oz) milk

1 Preheat oven to 250°C (450°F) Gas 7.
2 Rub the butter or margarine into the flour until it resembles fine breadcrumbs.
3 Add the dried fruit or grated cheese, then gradually stir in the milk.
4 Turn the dough onto a floured surface and knead lightly to remove any cracks.
5 Roll the dough out to a thickness of about 2 cm (¾ in).
6 Cut into shapes with a small biscuit cutter and place on a greased baking tray. Press all the trimmings together and roll out to make more scones.
7 Bake for about 10 minutes until well risen and golden brown.

WHOLEMEAL SPONGE WITH CAROB OR COCOA *(page 80)*

Ingredients
100 g (4 oz) soft margarine
100 g (4 oz) sugar
2 eggs, beaten
100 g (4 oz) wholemeal self-raising flour
1 tbsp carob or cocoa powder

1 Preheat oven to 180°C (350°F) Gas 4.
2 Line two 18 cm (7 in) sandwich tins with greased paper.
3 Cream the fat and sugar together until smooth and light.
4 Gradually mix in the eggs and flour, keeping the mixture smooth.
5 Divide the mixture in two and mix the carob or cocoa powder into one half.
6 Place alternate spoonfuls of the mixtures in the tins. Swirl with a knife several times to create a marbled effect.
7 Bake for 15–20 minutes until firm. Turn out onto a wire rack and leave to cool.

CARROT CAKE *(page 80)*

Ingredients
150 ml (5 fl oz) oil
100 g (4 oz) sugar
3 eggs, beaten
200 g (7 oz) flour
2 tsp bicarbonate of soda
1½ tsp ground cinnamon
4–5 large carrots, peeled and grated

1 Preheat oven to 150°C (300°F) Gas 2.
2 Grease a 23 x 32 cm (9 x 13 in) tin and line it with greased greaseproof paper.
3 Beat the oil into the sugar.
4 Add the eggs and beat well to mix.
5 Sift all the dry ingredients together and add to the wet mixture. Mix well.
6 Fold in the grated carrots.
7 Spoon the mixture into the tin and bake for about 1 hour until golden brown.

DATE AND NUT CAKE *(page 80)*

Ingredients
350 g (12 oz) dried dates, chopped
225 ml (8 fl oz) boiling water
275 g (10 oz) flour
1 tsp baking powder
1 tsp bicarbonate of soda
50 g (2 oz) sugar
65 g (2½ oz) nuts, finely chopped
75 ml (3 fl oz) oil
1 egg, beaten
1 tsp vanilla extract

1 Preheat oven to 180°C (350°F) Gas 4.
2 Grease and line a loaf tin.
3 Place dates in a bowl and pour over the boiling water. Stir and cool.
4 Mix the flour, baking powder, bicarbonate of soda, sugar and nuts.
5 Stir the oil, egg and vanilla into the cooled date mixture.
6 Add the wet mixture to the dry ingredients, stirring just to moisten them.
7 Spoon into the tin and bake for about 1 hour. Or fill small paper cases and bake for about 30 minutes until golden brown.

CHAPTER

SPECIAL OCCASIONS

As long as your child is eating and enjoying a healthy
diet most of the time, there is no reason to exclude
special treats on birthdays, holidays and festive occasions.
You can start early to develop good habits by encouraging
your child to appreciate less sickly treats than the
commercial confectionery, chocolates, cakes and biscuits
that are usually offered at such times. Experiment with
carob instead of chocolate, bake with wholesome
ingredients, and offer fresh and dried fruits instead of
sugar-laden and artificially coloured sweets. Healthy
habits learned in the first years will last a lifetime.

EASTER FEAST

Easter shouldn't be solely about Easter eggs. You can make it a special occasion with other festive foods and shapes such as those shown here. Even older children will be excited by this Easter bunny, which should divert their attention from the ubiquitous chocolate eggs. The open sandwich is topped with grated apple, carrot and cheese mixed with yoghurt and mayonnaise. Raisins and carrots provide the finishing touches. The curd-cheese egg is easily made by rolling a teaspoon of low-fat soft cheese between the palms of your hands. You can decorate it with chopped fresh parsley or ground nuts.

Easter bunny
Serve an appetizing spread of grated apple, carrot, cheese, yoghurt and mayonnaise on French bread, with soaked raisins for the bunny's eyes and carrot for its whiskers and ears.

Fruity chick with nest
This chirpy Easter chick is made from soaked dried apricot halves and pieces of fresh pineapple. A curd-cheese egg waits to hatch in a carrot, cucumber and courgette nest.

Shaped raw carrot

Soaked dried apricot

Soaked raisin

French bread

Fresh pineapple

Carrot, cucumber and courgette nest

Curd cheese

EASTER TREATS

Start early by developing good habits where chocolate is concerned, particularly at Easter when there is so much of it around. Do make it a time for special treats, but follow the ideas shown here to help cut down on the chocolate intake. Rather than offering pieces of solid chocolate, give your child fruit or cereal biscuits that have been dipped in melted chocolate. Alternatively, try using a carob bar instead of chocolate: your child might like the taste and it contains less fat and refined sugar.

CURD-CHEESE
EGGS DUSTED
WITH COCOA

DRIED APRICOT
DIPPED IN
CHOCOLATE

GRAPES DIPPED IN
MELTED CHOCOLATE

CAROB BISCUIT
(recipe p. 92)

PEANUT BUTTER
BALLS *(recipe p. 92)*

FRUIT TART
(recipe p. 73)

CAROB-DIPPED
STRAWBERRY

CHOCOLATE-DIPPED OATY
FLAPJACK *(recipe p. 63)*

CHOCOLATE-
DIPPED OAT BISCUIT
(recipe p. 62)

ICED YOGHURT
EGG *(recipe p. 92)*

CHRISTMAS DINNER

There is no reason why your child shouldn't share in the family's traditional Christmas dinner, perhaps including one or two special treats that you can prepare in advance, like this frozen yoghurt snowman. Since Christmas dinner tends to be a feast of rich, hearty foods, give your child only a small portion. Children are usually excited by the festive atmosphere and the decorations and may not have much of an appetite. Arrange their food enticingly in morsels so they can feed themselves and you have more time to relax with the family and enjoy your meal.

Iced yoghurt snowman
Decorate two iced yoghurt eggs with soaked dried apricots and sultanas for this snowman. *(Recipe p. 92)*

Christmas star
Arrange turkey breast, small roast potatoes, carrot strips and quartered sprouts into a traditional Christmas shape.

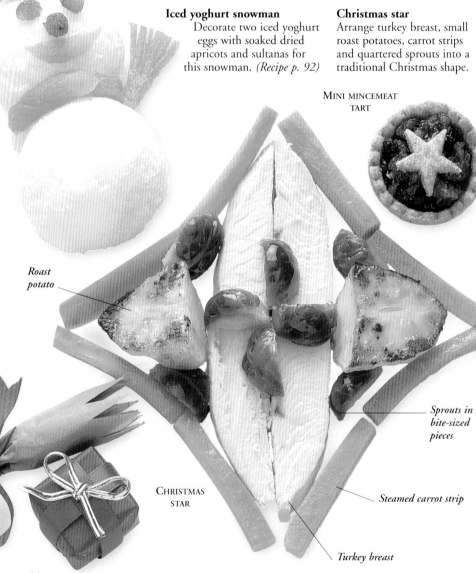

MINI MINCEMEAT
TART

Roast
potato

Sprouts in
bite-sized
pieces

Steamed carrot strip

CHRISTMAS
STAR

Turkey breast

CHRISTMAS TREATS

GINGERBREAD SANTA CLAUS *(recipe p. 93)*

For Christmas, you can prepare wholesome treats in advance and freeze or store them in airtight containers. A variety of tempting goodies can be made to replace the traditionally rich, high-fat, sugary Christmas fare. Invest in some seasonal biscuit cutters so you can produce festive and appealing shapes like this angel and bell. Try to use small pieces of fresh fruits in tarts to give them extra colour, and tone down rich mincemeat by adding chopped fresh apple or grated carrot to the fruit mixture before you fill and bake the pies in the oven.

GINGERBREAD ANGEL *(recipe p. 93)*

WHOLEMEAL ALMOND BISCUIT *(recipe p. 92)*

DESSERT OAT BISCUIT *(recipe p. 62)*

SHORTBREAD *(recipe p. 93)*

MINCEMEAT TART WITH APPLE

WHOLEMEAL FRUIT TART *(recipe p. 73)*

MINI PALMIERS *(recipe p. 92)*

DATE WITH RICOTTA CHEESE

BIRTHDAY PARTY

As long as children enjoy a healthy diet most of the time, there is no reason to exclude special treats on their birthdays and on other festive occasions. They may even come to associate such treats with special occasions only, and not demand or expect them every week. The most important thing about party food is its presentation. Most children are too excited to eat much, and you will want to cut down on your preparation time. So select a limited menu carefully and incorporate good healthy food wherever you can.

Birthday cake
For a wholesome and appetizing cake, follow one of the recipes and decorate with a topping of soft cheese, natural yoghurt and grated orange peel. *(Recipes pp. 63, 83 and 84)*

Finger salad
Fill a paper cupcake case with grated carrot, apple and beetroot. Decorate with a cherry tomato.

Tower sandwich
Layer wholemeal and white bread with sliced tomato, mustard and cress, curd cheese and chicken liver pâté. Cut in fingers to serve.

Open sandwich
To make these eye-catching and mouthwatering morsels, top small pieces of bread with fresh vegetables and firm cheese.

OPEN
SANDWICH

Mini quiche
Line tiny tartlet tins with pastry and fill them with a tasty custard made from eggs and cheese for this child-sized quiche in the shape of a narrow boat. *(Recipe p. 48)*

BOAT-SHAPED
QUICHE

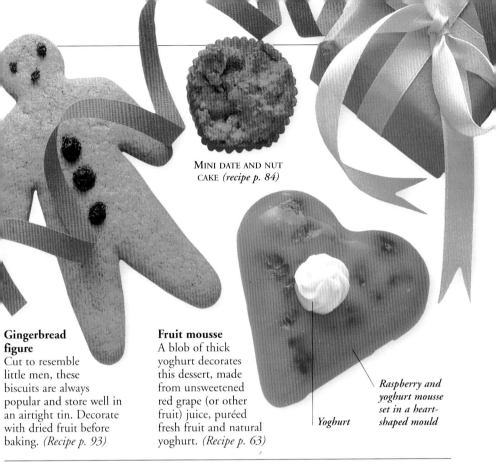

MINI DATE AND NUT CAKE *(recipe p. 84)*

Gingerbread figure
Cut to resemble little men, these biscuits are always popular and store well in an airtight tin. Decorate with dried fruit before baking. *(Recipe p. 93)*

Fruit mousse
A blob of thick yoghurt decorates this dessert, made from unsweetened red grape (or other fruit) juice, puréed fresh fruit and natural yoghurt. *(Recipe p. 63)*

Yoghurt

Raspberry and yoghurt mousse set in a heart-shaped mould

SWEETS AND TREATS

To forbid sweets completely is unrealistic. Allowing children unlimited amounts is also wrong. When babies are young, you won't have any problems with sweet-eating, but as children grow older they'll inevitably meet others who eat sweets without thinking. Try to be prepared for this by encouraging your child to appreciate less sickly treats and to accept sweet rationing and routines. If your child has a sweet treat with meals, it is less destructive for new teeth than having sweet snacks throughout the day. Get your child into the habit of cleaning teeth after every meal, and make it fun rather than a chore.

DATE CRUNCHY *(recipe p. 93)*

APRICOT AND ORANGE BALL *(recipe p. 93)*

ORANGE JELLY JUBE *(recipe p. 93)*

GRAPE-JUICE JELLY JUBE *(recipe p. 93)*

SPECIAL OCCASIONS RECIPES

CAROB BISCUITS *(page 87)*

Ingredients for 15–20 biscuits
100 g (4 oz) butter or margarine
50 g (2 oz) sugar
½ tsp vanilla extract
100 g (4 oz) flour, less 2 tbsp
2 tbsp carob powder

1 Preheat oven to 190°C (375°F) Gas 5.
2 Cream the butter or margarine and sugar together until light and fluffy. Mix in the vanilla extract.
3 Sift the flour with the carob powder and stir into the fat and sugar mixture.
4 Drop teaspoons of the mixture, well apart, onto a greased baking tray. Or chill the mixture to firm slightly, roll out and shape with small biscuit cutters. Bake the biscuits for 10–15 minutes, until hard.

PEANUT BUTTER BALLS *(page 87)*

Ingredients for about 15 pieces
100 g (4 oz) smooth peanut butter
50 g (2 oz) soaked raisins
175 g (6 oz) wheatgerm
40 g (1½ oz) dried milk powder
25 g (1 oz) ground nuts

1 Mix all the ingredients together and roll into balls or egg shapes.
2 Store in the refrigerator to help them stay firm and keep their shape.

ICED YOGHURT EGG *(page 87)*

Ingredients
350 ml (12 fl oz) natural yoghurt
175 ml (6 fl oz) orange juice
1 tsp grated orange peel

1 Mix all the ingredients well together.
2 Pour into a suitable container or into shaped containers for freezing.
3 Freeze until solid.
4 Use this recipe also for the Frozen yoghurt snowman (see p. 88).

WHOLEMEAL ALMOND BISCUITS *(page 89)*

Ingredients for 15–20 biscuits
175 g (6 oz) butter or margarine
100 g (4 oz) sugar
1 egg, beaten
100 g (4 oz) wholemeal flour
50 g (2 oz) ground almonds

1 Preheat oven to 180°C (350°F) Gas 4.
2 Cream the butter or margarine and sugar until light and fluffy.
3 Gradually mix in the egg.
4 Fold in the flour and ground almonds and mix well.
5 Spoon the mixture in small dollops, set close together to form circles, onto a well greased baking tray. Bake the biscuits for 10–15 minutes until lightly browned.

MINI PALMIERS *(page 89)*

Ingredients for 16 pieces
225 g (8 oz) frozen puff pastry, thawed
3 tbsp good-quality strawberry jam with
a high proportion of fruit

1 Preheat oven to 220°C (425°F) Gas 7.
2 Roll out the pastry on a floured surface into a long rectangle 6 mm (¼ in) thick.
3 Spread the whole pastry rectangle thinly with 2 tbsp of the jam.
4 Fold the long edges of the pastry in to meet at the centre and spread with the remaining jam. Fold the pastry in half lengthwise to hide the folds and form a narrow strip.
5 Firm the pastry down with your hand and cut into 6 mm (¼ in) slices with a sharp knife.
6 Place the slices on a dampened baking tray, cut sides down and well apart to allow the biscuits to spread.
7 Bake near the top of the oven for 10 minutes. Turn over and bake for a further 3–4 minutes until golden brown.

WHOLEMEAL SHORTBREAD
(page 89)

Ingredients for 10–15 pieces
 150 g (5 oz) butter or margarine
 175 g (6 oz) wholemeal flour
 50 g (2 oz) ground rice
 50 g (2 oz) sugar

1 Preheat oven to 160°C (325°F) Gas 3.
2 Beat the butter until thoroughly soft, then gradually work in the dry ingredients to make a stiff dough, using your hand or a wooden spoon.
3 Place the dough on a floured surface and knead lightly. Roll out to a thickness of about 6 mm (¼ in).
4 Cut into shapes or slices and place on a greased baking tray. Bake the biscuits for about 30 minutes, until tinged brown.

GINGERBREAD BISCUITS
(pages 89 and 91)

Ingredients for 15–20 biscuits
 350 g (12 oz) flour
 1 tsp bicarbonate of soda
 2 tsp ground ginger
 100 g (4 oz) butter or margarine
 100 g (4 oz) sugar
 45 ml (3 tbsp) molasses or black treacle
 1 egg, beaten

1 Preheat oven to 190°C (375°F) Gas 5.
2 Sift the flour, bicarbonate of soda and ginger together. Rub in the butter or margarine until the mixture resembles fine breadcrumbs. Stir in the sugar.
3 Warm the molasses or treacle until it is easy to pour. Make a well in the centre of the dry ingredients and add the treacle with the egg. Mix until well blended.
4 Turn the dough out onto a lightly floured board and knead lightly. Roll out to a thickness of about 6 mm (¼ in).
5 Cut out shapes and place, well apart to allow for spreading, on a lightly greased baking tray. Bake for about 10 minutes until golden brown.

APRICOT AND ORANGE BALLS
(page 91)

Ingredients for about 24 pieces
 450 g (1 lb) dried apricots, chopped
 1 medium orange, peeled and chopped
 65 g (2½ oz) grated coconut
 65 g (2½ oz) ground nuts

1 Mix all the ingredients together (mince them in a food processor, if possible).
2 Shape into balls and chill until firm.

JELLY JUBES *(page 91)*

Ingredients for about 20 pieces
 350 ml (12 fl oz) unsweetened fruit juice
 4 envelopes unflavoured gelatine or vegetarian substitute such as agar-agar
 2 tsp lemon juice

1 Heat the fruit juice but do not boil.
2 Dissolve the gelatine in a bowl standing over a saucepan of boiling water. Stir continuously until dissolved.
3 Stir the gelatine into the fruit juice and mix well. Remove from the heat and add the lemon juice.
4 Pour into a tray 10–20 mm (½–1 in) deep or into individual moulds. Allow to stand until firm. Cut jelly set in a tray into shapes, if desired. Store in the refrigerator.

DATE CRUNCHIES *(page 91)*

Ingredients for about 20 pieces
 100 g (4 oz) butter or margarine
 75 g (3 oz) chopped, stoned dried dates
 75 g (3 oz) dark brown sugar
 100–150 g (4–5 oz) sugar-free wholewheat breakfast cereal
 shredded coconut (optional)

1 Mix the butter, dates and sugar in a saucepan and cook over a low heat until the dates have softened.
2 Remove from the heat and mix in the breakfast cereal to make a stiff consistency.
3 Cool, then shape into balls.
4 Roll in coconut to decorate, if desired.

INDEX

A

allergies, 25, 27
almond biscuits, wholemeal, 89, 92
apricot and orange balls, 91, 93
avocados: stickman feast, 77, 83

B

balanced diet, 26, 28–29
banana oatmeal cake, 80, 83
beakers, 11, 16
beany ring, 66
beef: meat loaf motor car, 58, 62
  merry meatball pony, 57
  pick-up pasta boat, 61, 63
beefburgers: rattle munch, 59, 63
beetroot: borscht, 75
bibs, 11, 20
bird's nest feast, 65
birthday parties, 90–91
biscuits, 80
  carob biscuits, 87, 92
  gingerbread biscuits, 89, 91, 92
  oat biscuit dessert, 57, 62
  oaty flapjack tree, 60, 63
  plain oat biscuits, 41
  wholemeal almond biscuits, 89, 92
boats: egg sail-boats, 42
  pick-up pasta boat, 61, 63
  tuna potato boat, 52
booster seats, 10
borscht, 75
bowls, 11
bread, 38
  cornbread, 41
  sandwich man, 78
  wholewheat bread, 41
breakfast, 37–41
breastfeeding, 12
butter bean soup, 75
butterfly pastie, 51, 53
buying food, 30

C

cakes, 80
  banana oatmeal cake, 80, 83
  carrot cake, 80, 84
  date and nut cake, 80, 84
  wholemeal sponge, 58, 63
  wholemeal sponge with carob or cocoa, 80, 84
carbohydrates, 26, 28
carob biscuits, 87, 92
carrots: carrot cake, 80, 84
  carrot soup, 76
cars: fruit jelly car, 64, 72
  meat loaf, 58, 62
cat and mouse, 43
cat face omelette, 43, 48
cereals, 14–15, 17, 37
chairs: booster seat, 10
  clip-on chair, 10
  high chair, 10
cheese, 45
  cheesy monster, 44, 48
  smiley face pizza, 46, 48
chick peas: falafel ball eggs, 65, 72
  hummus, 79, 83
chicken: chicken chews, 55, 62
  chicken stock soup, 76
chocolate, 87
Christmas dinner, 88
Christmas treats, 89
clock face, breakfast, 39
cornbread, 41
cups, drinking from, 16
cutlery, 11

D E

dairy products, 14–15, 26–7
dates: date and nut cake, 80, 84
  date crunchies, 91, 93
digestive system, 12
dips, 79
dried fruit balls, 49, 53
drinks, 13, 14–15, 16
drop scones, 41
Easter feast, 86
Easter treats, 87
eating out, 23
eggs, 14–15
  cat face omelette, 43, 48
  egg sail-boats, 42
equipment for weaning, 10–11
  bibs and feeding utensils, 11
  kitchen equipment, 11

F

fads, 18
falafel ball eggs, 65, 72
fast foods, 23
fats and oils, 26–27
feeding problems, 24–25
fibre, 28
finger foods, 17, 18
fish, 14–15, 49–53
fish finger tree, 50, 53
food intolerance, 25
food mills, 11, 31
food poisoning, 30
food preparation, 30–31
fruit, 20, 34
  dried fruit balls, 49, 53
  food pyramid, 26
  fruit jelly car, 64, 72
  fruit mousse, 59, 63
  introducing, 14–15
  mixed fruit tart, 69, 73
  nutrients, 28
  pancake slices, 77, 83
  preparation, 31
  self-feeding, 17
fruit juice, 13, 16, 29
funny fish, 49, 53

G H I

gastroenteritis, 25
gingerbread biscuits, 89, 91, 92
gluten sensitivity, 25
guacamole, 83
high chairs, 10–11, 16
hummus, 79, 83
hygiene, 30
illness, 25

J K L

jelly: fruit jelly car, 64, 72
    jelly jubes, 91, 93
kitchen equipment, 11
kite, stir-fried, 70
lactose intolerance, 25
leafy parcel train, 68, 72–73
lentils: cheesy monster, 44, 48
    lentil soup, 76
liver log cabin, 60

M N

mealtimes, 22–23
meat, 14–15, 54–63
meat loaf motor car, 58, 62
meatball pony, 57
menus, 18, 21
messy eaters, 20–21
milk, 24
    lactose intolerance, 25
    nutrition, 26–27
    snacks, 29
    weaning, 12, 16
minerals, 28
mini palmiers, 89, 93
mini sandwiches, 81
mouse, pear, 43
mousse, fruit, 59, 63
nutrition, 26–29
nuts, 14–15, 20

O

oatmeal: banana oatmeal cake, 80, 83
    merry meatball pony, 57, 62
    oat biscuit dessert, 57, 62
    oaty flapjack tree, 60, 63
    plain oat biscuits, 41
octopus, polka-dot, 67
omelette, cat face, 43, 48
overweight children, 24

P

palmiers, mini, 89, 93
pancake slices, 77, 83
pasta boat, pick-up, 61, 63
pasties: butterfly pastie, 51, 53
    pastie crab, 54

pastry, 54
peanut butter balls, 87, 92
pears: butterfly pastie, 51, 53
    pear mouse, 43
peas: fresh pea soup, 75
pick-up pasta boat, 61, 63
picnics, 82
pizza, smiley face, 46, 48
polka-dot octopus, 67
pony, meatball, 57
potatoes: tasty teddy bear, 56, 62
    tuna potato boat, 52
prawns, jumping, 51
processed foods, 31
protein, 17, 20, 26, 28
pulses, 14–15, 66
purées, 31

Q R

quiche flower, 47, 48
rattle munch, 59, 63
refusal to eat, 25
reheating food, 30
restaurants, 23
rewards, 22
rice: rattle munch, 59, 63
rocket, vegetable, 69, 73

S

safety, food preparation, 30–31
salt, 7, 27, 36
sandwiches: mini sandwiches, 81
    sandwich man, 78
savoury cone, 71, 73
scones: drop scones, 41
    wholemeal scones, 80, 84
seeds, 14–15
self-feeding, 17
shortbread, wholemeal, 89, 93
smiley face pizza, 46, 48
smoked haddock: funny fish, 49, 53
snacks, 23, 25, 77–84
    planning, 29
soups, 74–76
spinach soup, 75
spoonfeeding, 12

stickman feast, 77, 83
stir-fried kite, 70
storing food, 30
sugar, 27
sunshine breakfast, 40
sweets: as rewards, 22
    healthy alternatives, 91, 93

T

tart, mixed fruit, 69, 73
teddy bear, tasty, 56, 62
teething, 19
tell-the-time breakfast, 39
toddlers, 20–21
tomatoes: fresh tomato soup, 75
    smiley face pizza, 46, 48
traffic lights, 64, 72
treats, 22, 87, 89, 91
tuna potato boat, 52
turkey: tasty teddy bear, 56, 62

V

vegetables, 20, 32–33
    food pyramid, 26
    introducing, 14–15
    leafy parcel train, 68, 72–73
    nutrients, 28
    preparation, 31
    quiche flower, 47, 48
    recipes, 64–73
    savoury cone, 71, 73
    self-feeding, 17
    soups, 74–6
    traffic lights, 64, 72
    vegetable rocket, 69, 73
vegetarian diet, 13
vitamins, 28

W Y

weaning, 12–15
wholemeal almond biscuits, 89, 92
wholemeal shortbread, 89, 93
wholemeal sponge, 58, 63
    with carob or cocoa, 80, 84
wholewheat bread, 41
yoghurt egg, iced, 87, 92

ACKNOWLEDGMENTS

Dorling Kindersley would like to thank the following individuals for their contribution to this book.

PHOTOGRAPHY
Photographs by Martin Brigdale, pages 37–91. All other photographs by Jules Selmes except Dave King, pages 10–11

HOME ECONOMISTS
Dolly Meers, Janice Murfitt

NUTRITION CONSULTANT
Karen Gunner

ADDITIONAL EDITORIAL AND DESIGN ASSISTANCE
Nicky Adamson, Claire Cross, Caroline Greene Maureen Rissik, Ruth Tomkins

INDEX
Hilary Bird

TEXT FILM
The Brightside Partnership, London